Katy Perry:
The Unofficial Biography

Alice Montgomery is a freelance author living and working in London. Writing under a pseudonym, she is the author of several bestselling biographies, including *Susan Boyle: Dreams Can Come True*.

Katy Perry

The Unofficial Biography

ALICE MONTGOMERY

MICHAEL JOSEPH
an imprint of
PENGUIN BOOKS

MICHAEL JOSEPH

Published by the Penguin Group

Penguin Books Ltd, 80 Strand, London WC2R ORL, England

Penguin Group (USA) Inc., 375 Hudson Street, New York, New York 10014, USA

Penguin Group (Canada), 90 Eglinton Avenue East, Suite 700, Toronto, Ontario, Canada M4P 2Y3
(a division of Pearson Penguin Canada Inc.)

Penguin Ireland, 25 St Stephen's Green, Dublin 2, Ireland (a division of Penguin Books Ltd)

Penguin Group (Australia), 250 Camberwell Road, Camberwell, Victoria 3124, Australia
(a division of Pearson Australia Group Pty Ltd)

Penguin Books India Pvt Ltd, 11 Community Centre, Panchsheel Park, New Delhi – 110 017, India

Penguin Group (NZ), 67 Apollo Drive, Rosedale, Auckland 0632, New Zealand
(a division of Pearson New Zealand Ltd)

Penguin Books (South Africa) (Pty) Ltd, 24 Sturdee Avenue,
Rosebank, Johannesburg 2196, South Africa

Penguin Books Ltd, Registered Offices: 80 Strand, London WC2R ORL, England

www.penguin.com

First published 2011

1

Copyright © Alice Montgomery, 2011

The moral right of the author has been asserted

Set in 13.5/16pt Garamond MT Std
Typeset by Jouve (UK), Milton Keynes
Printed in Great Britain by Clays Ltd, St Ives plc

A CIP catalogue record for this book is available from the British Library

HARDBACK ISBN: 978–0–718–15825–5
TRADE PAPERBACK ISBN: 978–0–718–15826–2

www.greenpenguin.co.uk

MIX
Paper from
responsible sources
FSC™ C018179

Penguin Books is committed to a sustainable
future for our business, our readers and our
planet. This book is made from paper certified
by the Forest Stewardship Council.

Contents

List of Illustrations

Her on-off relationship with Travis McCoy became increasingly tumultuous. (ABACA/Press Association Images)

Katy appeared on the Gym Class Heroes' video *Cupid's Chokehold*. (© AP/Press Association Images)

A natural beauty. (Jim Trifyllis/Newspix/Rex Features)

'California Gurl'. (© Press Association Images)

On stage at Vienna's life ball. (Karl Schoendorfer/Rex Features)

At the Hurricane Festival in Germany. (Action Press/Rex Features)

Performing on Italian *X Factor*. (MCP/Rex Features)

It's official. (Rex Features)

Not just a fling. (©ABACA/Press Association Images)

Katy has appeared in *FHM*'s 100 Sexiest Women poll twice. (© Press Association Images)

The happy couple at an awards ceremony after-party in LA. (*BDG*/Rex Features)

There were incredulous responses to the news that Lothario Russell Brand had married. (NBCUPHOTOBANK/Rex Features)

Katy and Russell's devotion to one another is obvious. (© Picturegroup/Press Association Images)

Enjoying a sky-high profile. (© Picturegroup/Press Association Images)

Santa Barbara, 1984

When a really big new star springs out of the show-business firmament, it's tempting to look back to their early childhood in order to find some clue as to what inspired their talent, drive to succeed and ability to stand out in a vastly competitive world. Sometimes the clues are there; sometimes they're not, but it's difficult to think of a single major pop sensation who's experienced the same kind of childhood as Katy Perry, which was happy, secure and seemed to set her up for life – though not as a controversial pop star married to an equally controversial comedian-turned-actor. The contrast between Katy's past and present couldn't be more stark.

Katheryn Elizabeth Hudson was born on 25 October 1984 in Santa Barbara, the middle child of three, with an older sister, Angela, and a younger brother, David. Katy's parents were once as flamboyant as their daughter: her father, Keith, now a pastor, moved in alternative circles on the West Coast of America in the 1960s, taking LSD and generally living hedonistically. He attended Woodstock, which at least showed him what to expect when his daughter turned out to be a pop star, and even played tambourine with Sly and the Family Stone. This all came to an abrupt halt, however, when he was in an apple orchard in

Wenatchee, Washington, where he had a revelation in which he saw passages from the Bible. While his daughter later commented that the vision might well have come about as a result of his drug use, Keith's path in life was set: he turned to religion and that has been his life ever since. He didn't do it half-heartedly either. The Hudson children were brought up very strictly, utterly protected from the harshness of the outside world, unable even to listen to pop music. The Christian world was their universe, and it wasn't until Katy left home — admittedly young — that she started to understand there was a very different life out there from the one she'd grown up with.

Mary, Katy's mother, grew up in southern California as part of a wealthy family in Santa Barbara, and had a very privileged background indeed. Her parents were Frank J. Perry, a stockbroker, and Pauline Schwab, who worked at Alcoholics Anonymous, while her uncle was Charles M. Schwab, who founded the Bethlehem Steel Corporation. While there was one minor showbusiness connection on her dad's side of the family — Keith's sister was a showgirl with the Folies Bergère — Mary's older brother, Frank, who died in 1995 aged sixty-five after contracting prostate cancer, was a stage and film director, producer and screenwriter, who's best remembered for directing the 1981 film *Mommie Dearest*, in which the actress Faye Dunaway put in a swivel-eyed performance as Joan Crawford.

Mary, too, had a pretty wild background before settling down. She was first married to a racing driver who'd lost a leg: the two of them moved to Zimbabwe, where they lived on a macademia-nut farm and after the marriage broke up, Mary went on to date Jimi Hendrix. Katy joked about this in later years, telling her mother she should have taken things further with Jimi, as then she, Katy, would have been a proper rock star. Mary then became a reporter, working at ABC radio, where she interviewed Jimmy Carter and Muhammad Ali. Mary met Keith when she was covering a tent revival – a gathering of Christian worshippers in a tent used for revival meetings, healing crusades and church rallies – and, like her husband, she went on to become a pastor, a move that led to an estrangement from her family. Katy later said that her mother's half-brothers disapproved of her decision to become a devout Christian, but that Mary was determined to choose the path that was right for her.

Keith and Mary's marriage was a happy one, and children soon started to come along. According to those closest to her, Katy was always an attention seeker. Her elder sister Angela said that Katy was always clamouring for attention, but despite this the siblings were close and their upbringing secure.

For people accustomed to a life of privilege, giving up the high life to dedicate themselves to God was a very big step. Nonetheless, Keith and Mary were totally committed to their ministry, even though money was extremely tight, so much so that at times the family came perilously close to the poverty line. On occasion they were forced to eat food intended for the congregation and the family often used food stamps. The children, of course, had never known anything different and were perfectly happy, although Katy did talk about this early hardship later on in her life.

Theirs was also a strangely nomadic existence, although this would prepare Katy for life on the road. When she was a child, the family moved constantly from one evangelist outreach to the next, everywhere from Florida to Oklahoma, before finally ending up in Santa Barbara. This meant constantly leaving school and friends behind and making new ones, and after a while not making new ones because she knew she was going to have to leave them again. It toughened Katy up, but it was an odd existence for a little girl, and it made her introverted. The only constants in the young Katy's life were her family and her religion, so increasingly she came to depend on them more and more. This in turn provided her with a bedrock of security that would help her as an adult.

Katy's home life wasn't just poor, it was extremely eccentric, too. 'I wasn't able to say I was "lucky", because my mother would rather us say that we were "blessed", and she also didn't like that "lucky" sounded like "Lucifer",' Katy told *Vanity Fair*. 'Even the Dirt Devil as a vacuum – didn't have one. Deviled eggs were called "angeled" eggs. I wasn't allowed to eat Lucky Charms, but I think that was the sugar. I think my mom lied to me about that one.'

Katy's parents' religion meant her upbringing was far more strict than you'd expect of a California girl turned slightly shocking pop star. Katy wasn't allowed to go to parties with boys, attend sex education classes in school or be exposed to television, films or popular culture. There was a fire and brimstone element to her childhood that taught Katy about Satan and hell and her life was kept strictly on the straight and narrow.

There was music around, just not the type Katy has become associated with. 'I was raised in a very pseudo-strict religious household where the only thing on the menu was "Oh Happy Day", "His Eye Is On The Sparrow" and "Amazing Grace" – all eight verses of it,' Katy told *MTV News* in June 2008. 'So the New Kids on the Block are new to me now; they're not a comeback. I'm like, "Oh, this is a cool song!" I missed out on a couple other things, but I'm catching up. That led to me being fourteen or fifteen when I started going to Nashville to record some gospel songs, and to be around amazing country-music vets and learn how to craft a song and play guitar. I'd actually have to Super Glue the tips of my fingers because they hurt so much from playing guitar all day, you know? And from that, I made the best record I could make as a gospel singer at fifteen.'

Katy's parents were clearly more eccentric than many preachers, however. Keith accumulated four tattoos, all of which said 'Jesus', and the family would regularly speak in tongues (sounds made by some Christians when they go into a trance-like state and which is thought to be a gift from the Holy Spirit). Katy grew up totally used to listening to people speaking in tongues and to regular prayer, and she was very devout herself, praying whenever she felt she needed divine help. God and Jesus were at the very centre of family life.

Right from the start, certain expectations were made of Katy. She wasn't just living in a very religious community, her parents were at the very heart of it and she was expected to behave accordingly, which she did. Whatever her fellow Christians made of her later career – and quite a few eyebrows have been raised – Katy has never rebelled against her parents, dabbled in drugs or gone down the route to self-destruction, and she maintains a healthy contempt for those who do.

Asked by Christian radio presenter and journalist Mike Rimmer about being a pastor's child she replied, 'You mean being polished, shiny and new with a little red ribbon on your head? I'm not really into the whole pastor's kids thing. I think a lot of pastor's kids, my age especially, use that, twist it and make an excuse so they can be brats. I think it's just lame, I think they just need to stand and be who they are. I heard a saying that "people will influence a person daily, hundreds of times" and that made me think wow! I could influence a person by just doing something, being aware of something or being somewhere. Being a pastor's kid isn't hard, it'll be hard if I get into trouble. I never really went through a rebellious phase like taking a lot of drugs or anything like that. I never went out and got drunk, messed around with guys. Your testimony can just be "Thank you God that I've never been there".'

Katy attended Christian schools and during the summer was sent to Christian summer camps, but from the age of nine it was clear she was extremely musical, which was encouraged by her parents, and as she got older she started learning how to dance, too. 'When I first started out, I was really attracted to having my own sense of style because I started swing dancing, Lindy Hop, and jitterbug. I would go to the Santa Barbara rec [recreation] hall and I would learn how to dance there,' she said in an interview with *Seventeen* magazine, in which she pointed out that these young experiences affected her style as an adult.

'I was taught by some of the more seasoned dancers who were actually very involved in the scene. These girls would get out of their old vintage Cadillacs with their pencil skirts and their tight little cardigans and their bullet bras and I thought it was so unique and different than what was going on in the 2000s. I think it's grown a lot – it's changed. I love details. I love different colors. I love funny things. I have this one shirt that's got smiley faces as shoulders – so it's really cute and quite humorous. I love a good sense of humor in clothes.'

When she was thirteen, Katy had her own personal conversion to Christianity. Obviously she had been brought up as a Christian, but now she began to make it personal to herself. Born-again Christians have to be just that, born again, and many children of evangelical parents feel the need to undergo their own entrance into the church, which is what happened to Katy at this point.

'I was one of those kids going to camp and every time there was an altar call I was there,' she told Mike Rimmer. 'I'm a pastor's kid, so I grew up knowing about Christ and Christianity and stuff like that. I didn't actually make it my own until I was going through a process when I was thirteen. It's becoming a more personalized faith to me daily because I actually realized that my parents weren't my salvation and they weren't the ones that were going to be judged and just because they're Christians and pastors doesn't make me shiny and new. Salvation is for everyone but you have to make it a personal choice. I came to a realization that I'm believing because I'm believing not because it's been thrown in my face all of these years. So basically I just have adopted it as my own faith and grown out of the mode of letting it be a family tradition. I knew that God had been knocking on the door for quite a while and God was the only one that truly understands me completely because I'm such an outcast and a kooky little, funky person.' This is one of the reasons that her fellow Christians have been so shocked by the later stages in her life.

Katy went on to attend Dos Pueblos High School, a very well-regarded institution in Goleta, just west of Santa Barbara. The school is a National Blue Ribbon School, the highest accolade that can be awarded to a school in the United States education system, and as well as having a highly regarded academic side – it offers the International Baccalaureate – there were plenty of extra-curricular activities, including performance arts, music and sport. In short, it was exactly the sort of school in which a talented, bright young student could thrive, which Katy did. Indeed, she began the first stage of her singing career in 2001, when she was still a student, although it would be many more years before she made the breakthrough that would make her name.

The school now runs an online site called DPMedia-Online, and in an interview to DPNews Katy said, 'My biggest goal at DP was that I wanted to be a singer. I wanted to be like Gwen Stefani and Alanis Morissette. I wanted to have some rock and roll angst of Shirley Manson from Garbage. I was always singing. I was never in one click [clique]; I would bop around to different clicks and take in what they were made of. Like, I was never part of the cheerleaders or the geeks or the thespians or the outcasts. I was hanging out with all of them. I was a little social butterfly. Also it made me really appreciate differences.

'I wasn't the best student. My grades weren't perfect, but they were good. And my parents were still watching out. I knew there were some subjects I was better in than others. I loved history. I wanted to know where I came from, I wanted to know art history, because it influenced my music or the potential visual I was going to have in the future. I was really into English because it helped me write better songs. I was really into anything activity-wise, because there was a team player thing which you need when you're on the road and you've got a lot of people and it works better on a team.'

In September 2010, after she'd become famous, Katy returned to perform at the school, where many of the teachers who'd taught her still worked. 'Mr Jacobs, my choir master!' she exclaimed, as she saw the waiting teachers and students. Katy was quite overwhelmed when she heard he had turned up in the crowd to see her. Then she saw Mr Mitchell, her history teacher. 'He used to make fun of me!' she said. 'He'd say, "You're going to be a singer? Do your homework!" And I was, like, "I'll show you one day, Mr Mitchell." And I did!'

She delighted the assembled crowd when she recognized one of their number. 'Is that Shane Lopes?' she cried. 'You were the most popular kid in my class, but you never wanted to date me, it was always Amanda Wayne. Oh yeah, you really chose right, honey. What's up now, playa?'

Shane had been a high school (American) football star in Goleta, and played quarterback at Delaware State before returning to his home town to coach the high school team. In the wake of Katy's very public announcement, he was a little embarrassed and his comments to Radar Online throw some light on the truth behind the comment. 'That whole story is pretty fabricated,' he said. 'I never got the feeling that she had a crush on me. We've always been friends. I think it was more for entertainment and she was figuring out a way to segue into her next song and kinda embarrass me just for fun. I didn't expect it [to be singled out in the crowd], but I wasn't shocked because that's just her personality. She's always been that way – very outspoken, goofy and she's just a funny girl. It's no different than the Katy I knew before. I can speak for the rest of the class when I say we all knew she had a gift, so I wasn't surprised when she came out with a hit. Not everyone can say they know someone that famous, but with her personality and talent I remember thinking to myself when I was younger, "Maybe she has a chance, maybe it's a star in the making."'

While she was at school, religion was never far from her mind. 'I was wondering how people would change and shape up if Christ was here attending my school,' she told *7 Ball* magazine in an interview when she was sixteen. 'I was like, If Jesus came back as a simple high school kid, how would you act in front of Him? I want people to understand that it hurts Christ when they ignore Him and live their lives. The pain is like crucifying Him again and again.'

Katy had a lot of secular influences as well. Although she was to speak at length about the fact that she and her siblings were barely allowed to listen to anything other than Christian music, at the age of thirteen she caught a glimpse of the hugely flamboyant Freddie Mercury, which made a massive impression on her. 'He seemed to have come on stage like a firecracker,' she recalled many years later. 'And I love that. He was an entertainer. You know? And that's what I want to be, is an entertainer.'

She was a lively girl right from the start. At a pool party once, one of the boys dared the girls to jump off a roof. None of the girls took him up on it except Katy, who to this day has a scar on her ankle to show for it.

By the time Katy reached her early teens, it was becoming apparent that she had a real talent musically so, at the prompting of her parents, she began to take singing lessons, although it wasn't initially clear where this would lead. A myth has grown up around what happened next, as it's been widely reported that she briefly enrolled in the Music Academy of the West in Santa Barbara. It's a summer school and festival and one of its eight-week programmes was reported to be Katy's first step towards deciding that music would be her long-term career. The programme supplied proper, formal training of a kind that Katy had lacked until then, exploring a wide range of vocal techniques including, to the bemusement of some of her fans, Italian opera (footage of her singing this still exists on YouTube).

The reality is somewhat different, according to Tim Docherty, who works at the Academy. 'Katy was never involved in our programme,' he said. 'She was never a fellow, as we call our students. We are one of the most prestigious music schools on the West Coast, inviting vocalists from all over the world. What actually happened was that she might have taken a music lesson from rooms we rent out.' There's no suggestion that Katy herself was responsible for the story, but it certainly didn't hurt her musical credentials to be associated with the school.

Meanwhile Katy's formal education was coming to an end. It's unclear whether she dropped out and whether or not she obtained her GED (General Education Diploma, the standard measure of a completed pre-university education in the United States), although it seems she left at the end of her freshman (first) year. It was early, but something had to give. It would have been impossible to pursue a full-time education while building a singing career and Katy had to choose.

Katy's talent was such that she was beginning to attract attention from further afield. She regularly sang in church and on Christian television, and it was on one of those occasions that veterans from the music industry in Nashville, Tennessee heard her. With its Grand Ole Opry House, Nashville is the centre of the US country music scene and it's also an important centre for gospel music. When Katy was about fourteen, she travelled to Nashville, where she started learning about other aspects of her future trade. She learned how to play the guitar and write songs, and she even began to record some tracks. All the time she was surrounded by some of the most talented, best-known musicians in the country music scene, making it an ideal time for her to shape her musical direction.

This was also the first time Katy had been properly exposed to mainstream music. Until then, her entire life had been focused on the church, so much so that she'd been utterly clueless about any other sort of music. Inevitably, perhaps, this meant that her first musical forays were with gospel, although she was starting to take an interest in other types of music as well.

'I picked up a Carman track. That's honest. "River of Life" by Carman,' she told Christian Music Central in an interview back in 2001, explaining how she started out. 'That's all I ever grew up on was Christian music. Picked it up, because my sister started singing, and I copied every little thing she did. It was actually her tape, but I stole it. So I took it and I practiced it and I performed it before she did. And my parents got me lessons, and then around thirteen, I just got focused. That's why I am here today, because my parents . . . But I really started getting serious when I was thirteen, and the church gave me a guitar, and writing songs, because I was so fed up with everyone being like, "Oh, I'm fifteen and I have something that I have to say." And I'm like, "Really? Then write it! If you have something to say, you sure as well can write it." And that's all I have to say. And goodnight!'

That was the confidence of youth speaking out, but Katy has always been confident. Coming from an utterly secure and stable family background, Katy grew up grounded, knowing she was loved and encouraged to make the best use of her talents. Her parents were thrilled about what was happening to her, and more than that, they gave her the freedom to explore this new path. During the early days, however, it wasn't easy: Katy was still at school at this point, and so far there had been no talk of her dropping out, so she had to fit her nascent musical career around her school work. It required a very disciplined approach, but Katy was good at discipline, and it would prove extremely good training for her future career.

Although her breakthrough was still some years away, Katy was already beginning to attract some media attention, albeit mainly from Christian news sites and magazines. She had the talent, all right, but she also had something even more important: star quality. Interviews from that era reveal an enormously confident girl who wasn't afraid to speak her mind and who wasn't nervous about what fate had in store. Despite the fact that she was mixing with famous, established musicians, she held her own and failed to be intimidated. Katy was starting to stand out in a crowd of aspiring hopefuls, for there were plenty of other talented teens in Nashville, hoping for their big break, most of whom would, of course, fall by the wayside, never to be heard of again. Not Katy, though, because she had a quality the others did not.

In more recent years – for she has served a long apprenticeship – Katy has talked about her religious upbringing and relationship with God, which, she would be the first to say, still exists. Back in those early days, though, religion dominated her life in a way that it doesn't seem to now, and that includes her music. Katy originally saw herself as picked by God to make music and share the message – she saw it as a voyage of understanding herself through Christianity. At that stage, everything in her life led to God and everything she had came from God. Now that we're in the Russell Brand era of Katy's life it's easy to forget that, but back then God totally defined who she was.

As Katy began to record some numbers and do the odd performance, people started to take notice of her. At the time she gave some interviews that reveal her state of mind back then. 'What I get out of writing songs are a release, comfort, understanding, and a better knowledge of who I am in Christ, and who God wants me to be,' Katy said in an interview with a Christian website. 'It's kind of like questions and cries and calls – all my songs are about my life – and most of them about my disappointments, because I just have way too many of them to write anything happy. I'm kidding. I'm not like that. But, I mean, people inspire me . . . But writing and stuff like that – that's just living my life. God influences me completely. Just taking some time to go chill and be quiet and listen and think about everything.'

That religion was so important to her comes as a surprise to her more recent fans, but it shouldn't. Nashville isn't just the home of the Grand Ole Opry; it has its fair share of evangelical churches, too. There's also a tradition in the United States of popular singers coming from gospel backgrounds and there's a strong link between worship and song. Elvis Presley, to take one noted example, was deeply influenced by his religious background, recording three gospel albums between 1960 and 1971 and never entirely relinquishing his connection to the church and his faith. In other countries, it's perhaps more difficult to understand the depth of the link, but it was Katy's religious background that was turning her into a star as much as her determination and talent.

In this crucially formative period of her life, Katy was beginning to learn her trade in other ways, too. She had been performing in public for years now, at school and more recently in Nashville, but there's a big difference between a school choir and a public concert. Katy had her first taste of touring at the age of sixteen, appearing on Phil Joel's Strangely Normal Tour. While not quite yet the polished performer she went on to become, it was obvious that she had stage presence and the ability to work with an audience. She was popular with her fellow performers as well, for her liveliness and charm: on tour in strange cities she would curtsey to passing policemen, joke with them and sometimes even play with their gun. In some ways, this could be seen as an apprenticeship period, although it didn't all go as smoothly as planned.

Katy's youth showed through in some of these tours, however, especially when you bear in mind that she was playing to Christian audiences. 'She had a beautiful voice, but she would sometimes say things that would shock some of the older people,' recalled Anna McGukin Hamilton, a road manager on one of these early tours. 'I'd be like, "OK, maybe you should have edited that one, Katy."' One example was Katy's habit of referring to God as 'Dude':

'I was talking to God last night and I said, "Dude, can you help me with so and so?"' The audiences would sometimes look rather stiff at this.

Katy continued to hold her own alongside far bigger names, becoming a regular at the Douglas Corner Café in Nashville on songwriter night, no less, where she started to win round grizzled music veterans with songs she'd written at the age of fifteen. Songwriter night was a prestigious evening, when experienced songwriters performed the latest hits they'd written. On one such night, when Katy sang 'Search Me', the audience exploded in approval, much to the chagrin of the considerably older music scene veteran who was due to perform next. 'That just makes me mad,' he said teasingly. 'How old are you again? That's not fair.'

Katy was, indeed, pretty young, but the time for her to start pursuing her music career full time was fast approaching, and to do that she would have to move properly to Nashville, half the country away from California. Her parents, so protective of their brood, were concerned, but they also wanted what was best for their daughter, and so, when still not much more than a child herself, Katy left home aged sixteen.

Katy Hudson

When Katy Hudson first arrived in Nashville she had nowhere to stay. Her family couldn't help out – they were hundreds of miles away – so she began a peripatetic existence, sleeping on friends' sofas. There was no alternative as there certainly wasn't enough money to pay the rent on an apartment.

When Katy was still just sixteen, she signed her first record contract with Red Hill Records to release her first offering, titled simply *Katy Hudson*. She had very high expectations about what was to come, though she was canny enough to realize that it was crucial, in building a fan base, to get the content right. 'Your first CD, honestly, has to appeal to a wide audience, because you've gotta build that fan base,' she told a Christian website. 'You can't just be in that genre that's just secluded to a fan base of like 15,000 people in the world, who are the only people that like that kind of music. That's cool if you wanna do that, but that's not what a record label has in mind. If your heart's there, then that's for you and not for a label.'

Red Hill would have seemed, from the outside, to be the perfect place for Katy to go. In 1995, the Oregon-based businessman and philanthropist Robert B. Pamplin Jr founded Pamplin Music, an independent Christian record label that was part of the already established Pamplin Entertainment and Pamplin Communications empire, a Christian media group comprising newspapers, radio stations and, briefly, a record label. Pamplin made its way into the top five Christian music record labels, focusing on pop, soft rock and R&B, whilst also creating several sub-labels to cater for different audiences. Organic Records was set up for alternative and modern rock artists; Cathedral Records and Crossroads were for the gospel market and Red Hill Records was for the youth market. Its artists and development were to be handled by Dan Michaels, who had made his name with the alternative Christian rock band The Choir.

With hindsight, it's possible that Katy simply wasn't ready. She wasn't polished enough, and although she had talent, it wasn't being channelled in the right direction. 'Katy was kind of a diamond in the rough,' said Tommy Collier, who co-produced and co-wrote two songs for the album. 'You could tell she was gonna be an expensive race car, but she didn't know how to drive it yet.'

In the meantime, Katy's housing problems had been temporarily solved. Now aged seventeen, she met twenty-four-year-old Mandy Collinger-Parsons, who now runs a Christian music PR company in Franklin, Tennessee. Back then Mandy was doing some work for Katy's record label, and when the two met, they hit it off and Mandy offered her a place to stay. They shared an apartment for three months, and Mandy met Katy's friends and her then boyfriend Justin.

'She was very full of life, animated and talkative,' she recalls. 'She was a ball to be around. She exuded energy. In fact, she was a bit of a loose cannon, somewhat raw. She was articulate, but not in the way she should be: she wasn't comfortable in an interview session and she wasn't focused. She would talk like she was thinking: in a stream of consciousness. She didn't really know how to behave.' Some of it was just gaucheness: Katy would burp in the middle of an interview, not realizing how it put people off.

On a professional level, Katy was going to require many hours of coaching, having her performances videoed and played back to her continually before she became the polished product she is today. Whilst there is no doubt that from the start she had a strong, resonant voice, during performances she often went off on a tangent while talking to the audience, ending up doing a twenty-minute monologue in between songs, which wasn't what anyone wanted to hear. She certainly wasn't a natural on stage, and it took a lot of intensive coaching before she began to improve.

Meanwhile, many hundreds of miles away, Katy's parents watched anxiously from the sidelines. At least they knew she was settled and living with a respectable fellow Christian, as they had talked to Mandy on the telephone to ensure their daughter had found a suitable place to live. Knowing that she was set on being a singer, Mandy believes that Katy's parents thought that entering the Christian music business rather than the more mainstream music industry was the best way to go. Even Katy's road manager was a Christian. The morals the Hudsons had inculcated in their daughter were very much in evidence at this time: there was no wild behaviour on Katy's part. She wore a cross, carried the Bible and, in Mandy's words, imposed her own curfew on herself. No one was telling her what to do, but Katy didn't go wild at all hours of the day and night. There wasn't much staying up late.

As for Katy and Justin, from what Mandy saw they were a pretty chaste couple. 'They would just sit on the couch and hold hands,' Mandy recalls. 'She was good, moral, always wanted to be respectable. Maybe these rules had been established at home, but she was really straight-laced. Justin would come round and play the guitar – it was a very sweet and innocent relationship. Her friends were in the Christian music industry: there was no drinking or party-ing.' No wonder, then, that Mandy, like many people from Katy's life at the time, couldn't believe it when she heard that Katy had got together with Russell Brand.

Whatever her drawbacks as an artist in the early days, Katy was clearly a loving friend. Mandy remembers that Katy didn't have a car back then and constantly relied on friends for a ride. On one occasion Mandy agreed to drive her to see Justin taking part in a 'battle of the bands'. On her way there, Mandy was involved in a serious car acci-dent and came round in the emergency ward to find herself surrounded by close relatives and a distraught Katy, who blamed herself. 'She was crying, saying, "It's all my fault that it happened,"' says Mandy.

'She was so loving and sweet and endearing. A lot of the

time we'd just go for rides, do things together – and because I was older I felt a responsibility to be a good example for her. I remember, she loved Love Spell perfume by Victoria's Secret. She would get dressed up and fix her make-up and perfume and looked super cute. She had no money to spend on clothes, so she'd get things in thrift stores, but she had a way of putting things together that looked amazing. She had charisma and presence even then.'

That first gospel album, *Katy Hudson*, is now a collectors' item and features ten tracks, including one called 'Trust In Me', which was the lead single, released on 6 March 2001. The others were 'Piercing', 'Search Me', 'Last Call', 'Growing Pains', 'My Own Monster', 'Split', 'Faith Won't Fail', 'Naturally' and 'When There's Nothing Left'.

Katy set up a website, also called Katy Hudson, to help promote the album and explain her thinking behind the songs. The first track, 'Trust In Me', clearly meant a great deal to her. 'This was my first try at songwriting,' she wrote. 'I was feeling a little depressed at the time, and was thinking about all the things I'd done wrong. I felt like I was oil and God was water, and I just wouldn't mix. I started writing about this and God placed a peace in my heart. I really felt He was saying, "Don't worry, child, trust in me." I just had to open my heart to the healing process.'

'"Piercing"', she said, 'is an aggressive song because I hate how people are so blinded by the so-called "necessities" of life, when truly nothing on this earth will ever satisfy you. I wanted to write a song about how people are so infatuated with the things of this world. We wrote about how everyone is so blinded with what they want, but they don't know what they really need.'

And so it went on: a mixture of the personal and the spiritual as Katy tried to explore both her faith and her role in life as a teenage girl. The songs are a world away from the light-hearted pop she's become famous for, portraying a depth and yearning for the more spiritual aspects in life. In some ways, of course, such solemnity is typical of a teenager trying to understand what life is about, but it was an impressive debut in many ways all the same.

The only problem was that the album didn't gel. Those reviewers that did notice it were generally favourable, but they were few and far between. In an extraordinarily competitive industry, Katy hadn't succeeded in producing a record that stopped the world in its tracks, and even her choice of record label eventually proved unfortunate. Later, critics called the album more 'angst' than pop.

On the album, Katy is credited as having written four of the songs by herself whilst co-writing the other six. Second-hand editions are still available on Amazon – with a starting price of around $80! – but it wasn't the smash debut Katy had hoped for and it would be many more years before she finally got the breakthrough she craved.

For those few who picked up on it, though, Katy acquitted herself perfectly well. Russ Breimeier reviewed it on the Christianity Today International website, realizing that hers was a talent worth commenting on. Tellingly, however, he starts the review by pointing out that Katy Hudson is a sixteen-year-old gospel singer and not Kate Hudson, the twenty-one-year-old actress daughter of Goldie Hawn. The performers' shared name went on to become an issue, and is the main reason Katy changed her name to Perry.

'Although her lyrics aren't quite brilliant, they're definitely insightful and well matched to the emotional power of Katy's music,' Breimeier wrote. 'Likewise, her music is very similar to what you would expect on your local modern pop/rock station (with the exception of "Growing Pains", which has a very unusual sound), but it's good enough to catch your attention. Katy Hudson's debut easily could have been just another teen songwriter mimicking mainstream music trends with Christian lyrics. Instead, I hear a remarkable young talent emerging, a gifted songwriter in her own right who will almost certainly go far in this business. That name again is Katy Hudson. Trust me, you'll be hearing it more and more in the next year.'

He was certainly right about Katy's potential, although he was a little over-optimistic about how fast her career would take off. Katy did her best to support the CD, giving a few early interviews, such as those quoted above, and opening for a variety of artists, including the American-Australian folk musician Jennifer Knapp, who was a major early influence and something of a mentor, but matters weren't helped when Red Hill went under and the record and single stopped being produced. It would be wrong to call Katy's first album a flop, but it certainly failed to make a splash.

Years later, however, it garnered a huge amount of interest, and not only because Katy had gone from singing gospel to something more risqué. She was clearly becoming a major star with lasting power, someone who was destined to endure the course, and this debut album wasn't just interesting because of her early evangelistic Christianity, but because it said something about her development as an artist.

Ironically, it wasn't until years after the record's release that it got the attention Katy had courted back then. 'To her credit, Perry never seems comfortable with that onslaught of sound – she starts scatting whenever she can and seems drawn to numbers that are a bit more playful (how else to explain her bizarre British accent on "Growing Pains"), so it's clear that this city girl would never be satisfied by sticking around down on a Christian farm,' wrote the critic Stephen Thomas Erlewine. 'But as an album, *Katy Hudson* is only instructive as the first act in a prefab pop star's career, to show that she has talent but that she was mismarketed – and that she couldn't quite fit as a Christian singer, either, so everybody is better off with Katy tasting cherry chapstick instead of communion wine.' It's a slightly glib comment that underestimates the strength of Katy's religious convictions back then.

Although it was a blow, Katy was still young, so it wasn't the disaster it might have been had it happened to an older woman. 'It wasn't a big label,' says Mandy Collinger-Parsons. 'If one of the major labels had been behind it, she might have got the pull and material support she needed. Her label didn't have the resources to develop her: you usually need three or four albums to break a new artist and she only had one. But when it went wrong, I don't know if she was that surprised. She was so young, and for her the sky was still the limit. She felt she could go anywhere as a new artist.' In retrospect, Mandy points out that there were very few Christian female singers around at the time, and that no one knew exactly what to do with Katy. Her quirkiness and individuality didn't really help back then, either, although it certainly did in the future. 'I think she was a prodigy,' says Mandy. 'She was just way ahead of her time.'

Meanwhile Katy had the opportunity to learn a great deal by working with some of the most important artists in her field, such as Jennifer Knapp. Unlike Katy, Jennifer hadn't been brought up in a religious family, but had converted to Christianity while attending Pittsburgh State University. Her faith came out repeatedly in the music she made and her first album, *Kansas*, released in 1998, was both a critical and commercial success, selling over 500,000 copies in total.

Katy toured and worked with Jennifer. 'I was on the road with her for a few days,' she said in an interview given at the time while she was opening for Jennifer. 'I don't get to talk to her a whole lot, 'cause she's been on this Bebo Norman, Justin McRoberts deal on tour. But when I do talk to her it's like she's my mentor. She's the one that's showing me the law of the land. Just totally showing me what to do and not to do. Just being total mentor, total influence, and I'm just sitting by the sidelines listening, and taking it all in . . . I'm just like, I'm here along for the ride, and the ride can be as important as playing, because you get to see everything that goes on. You really have to learn. Everyone is like, "Well, living on the road you have such a hard life, and it's such a free life." You have to learn a lot. It's a lot of like getting your priorities straight, time management and things like that. Because if you don't have that on the road, oh, everything just falls underneath you.'

Jennifer was to become more than just a mentor to Katy: along with Alabaster Arts president Steven Thomas, she became Katy's manager for a short while. This was something Katy's parents were very keen on. Their daughter had been toughened up by her nomadic experiences as a child, but she had also been sheltered by her parents and her Christian faith. Given their own early wild years, the Hudsons were all too aware of the kind of temptation that lay ahead, and they were keen for a responsible Christian woman like Jennifer to take Katy under her wing. The timing was right: Steven had managed Jennifer and the two were now partners in a management company, and Katy seemed like the right sort of person to take on.

'We have waited two years to find the right artist,' Steven told 7 *Ball* magazine in 2003. 'Katy has the right combination of talent and heart. We hesitated to sign a teenager, but Katy pulled us by our heartstrings from the very beginning. We believe that she has staying power, primarily because she's a strong songwriter and she connects well with a live audience.'

Katy's age had been an issue, however. She was still extremely young, and aside from the temptations of life on the road, successful recording artists come under a huge amount of pressure. If she did make it, would it destroy her? The terrible fate of Michael Jackson, still alive at the time and odder than ever, was a constant reminder to everyone in the music industry about what can happen if too much pressure is put on too narrow shoulders. There was also the issue of whether Katy would manage to achieve success at all. It was an awful burden for such a young woman, and initially Jennifer was very concerned about it.

'Katy is a really volatile subject for me personally,' Jennifer said to *7 Ball* at the time. 'There are like a ton of sub-eighteen-year-old artists out there. Frankly, I think Katy is talented. She is a wonderful personality. She has a great voice. She has a bright future. But Steve Thomas and I had a really hard time going, I don't know if I want to get into this. I don't agree, for lack of a better term, with pimping an artist to sell records.

'We've had a hard time deciding whether to be involved with an artist like Katy. Katy already had a record made and a marketing plan before we got in there. So [we're involved] hopefully to have an opportunity to impact her personally and her ministry. The issue is whether we are going to invest in it now and take the ridicule of having signed a young artist or allow her to take some other avenue without someone who cares for her. It sounds egotistical to think we will be able to do that but I will consider ourselves failures if we don't do that for her. We're not set up to make money. We said, Okay, you are going to finish school. We want her parents to call the shots. We're not really trying to take over the world with her. I think that's a couple of years off – I'd like her to be able to vote first!'

In the event, none of this would go according to plan. Jennifer and Steven's concern for Katy was beyond doubt, but there were just too many issues for everyone to deal with at the time. For starters there was the fact that her record label had shut down. Secondly, the album hadn't really been thought through commercially. Jennifer might have expressed doubts about making money out of Katy and expressed an admirable wish not to exploit her, but if Katy didn't make an impact, she wouldn't get heard. Ultimately, Katy was only going to find real success once she went mainstream, and it would be years before that would happen.

Not that Katy was ready for success back then. Her faith was so all-consuming that it didn't leave room for a mainstream commercial career, whatever she might have thought. At the time she was still immersed in gospel and wouldn't have liked or been happy performing mainstream pop. Looking back, it's also possible to say that early fame, especially at her age, might have destroyed her. Jennifer's very reasonable concerns were based on fact: many a promising young star has gone under after finding success too young. Frustrating as it was, Katy's relative lack of success at an early age might well have been her saving grace.

Katy's youth could have had the potential to cause problems in other ways, too. She wasn't just a practising Christian, she saw her musical career as a way of communicating God's message, but wasn't she too young to be telling an older audience about Christianity? She didn't think so. 'You know, "Growing Pains" is about me and give us some credit at my age,' Katy said at the time. 'I think sometimes I do struggle with that, because I have different audiences. Like, next week for GMA week, it's gonna be a tough cookie, because I'm gonna be playing in front of all these older people that have seen it all. They just sit back, hands folded, like, "show me what you've got." I don't like that. I like to help out, and kinda minister to the people. It'll be a little weird, but I'll hopefully just stay focused and remember that God doesn't put an age limit to a willing vessel. Basically, if you have the Bible to back it up, what are they gonna argue with?'

The fact that she was so young, of course. The Christian message was so important to Katy that she couldn't see her career in terms of anything else. Her intensity was such that her work was everything, and she couldn't understand why anyone would think it was *too* important to her.

'My songs are my life,' she continued. 'It's like a journal, it's my diary. I know somebody out there would be willing to listen to it. I'm trying to be as honest and blatant as I possibly can without scaring everybody. We as Christians like to beat around the bush so much. It's gonna have hard times. Nobody ever said it was gonna be easy. It's just life and you gotta deal with it. You always have someone that's gonna be critiquing you, and not liking things, and just a little analystic [sic] about it. But, you don't have to live for those people. You don't live for your audience – you live for God. For me, what I get out of my live shows – I don't care if I please my whole audience, because I know you can't please the world. If I'm speaking to four or five people directly, and they're being affected, and they're having a spiritual release with God right then and there, then I'm just all over that.'

The sentiments were admirable, but a rethink was required. Katy was a naturally pretty girl, but she was working in an industry where it's not enough to be pretty, you must be perfect. Attention started to focus on her appearance in a way it hadn't done in the past, and the attention wasn't straightforward. Katy was reaching her late teens – a time when girls like to experiment with make-up, try out looks and work out what suits them best – but that's a lot more difficult to do in the spotlight. She began to complain that if she wore black nail polish she was criticized for it. She wanted to work out who she was without having to do so in front of the world.

Katy had pinned her hopes on her debut album, and after all the excitement it had come to nought. Failure is a difficult thing to handle at any age, and after all those big hopes and plans, matters had come to an unceremonious halt. Katy had been touted as the next big thing, and now she seemed to have moved from 'the girl to watch' to 'yesterday's hero'. It would have been difficult for anyone to handle, but for a young teenager from a sheltered background it was even more difficult.

However, Katy is a pragmatist, and she still had her family and her faith providing rock-solid support. It wasn't over yet. Asked by one interviewer what had been her greatest challenge to date, Katy replied, 'Having expectations, and having them be broken one after another. Well, I have really high expectations of what I think should be – what I think should happen with an artist in the industry. You find out that a lot of things aren't always what they seem.'

Katy had found that out the hard way. She might have been an acclaimed performer on Nashville's music scene, something of a child prodigy even – the girl with the album deal, years ahead of her time – but the record had failed, the record company had gone bust, people were beginning to criticize her appearance and it was extremely hard to see where she would go from here. A lesser person would have given up, but not Katy.

She was, however, going to need all her inner resources over the next few years, as well as all the support and backing of her family, all the talent, self-belief and determination it was possible for her to access from deep inside. Katy has a strong character, but even so, the next few years weren't going to be easy. She was going to pay her dues over and over again before she finally got noticed on the national stage.

Katy sat back and took stock of her situation. Despite all that early hope and promise, she was going to have to start pretty much from scratch. Years of work and slog lay ahead, years of recordings that never made it off the ground, rejection and unhappiness. In the time-honoured tradition of the entertainment industry, it was going to take Katy the best part of a decade before she finally made her breakthrough and became an 'overnight success'!

The Dark Years

Glen Ballard was excited. The songwriter and record producer was just nudging fifty and a veteran of the rock scene, having worked with some of the most famous names in the business. Not only had he produced Michael Jackson's bestselling albums *Thriller* and *Bad*, he'd worked with Barbra Streisand, Quincy Jones, The Pointer Sisters, Paula Abdul, Alanis Morissette – who he effectively discovered – Anastacia, Annie Lennox and others too numerous to mention. Now he'd got wind of a promising new act – a seventeen-year-old singer called Katy Perry, although that wasn't the name she used yet.

The fact that Glen knew who Katy was is entirely down to Katy herself. Still licking her wounds from her early disappointments, she had decided that music was still where her future lay, so it was time to reassess. Although still a practising Christian, Katy began to think about signing with a more mainstream record label and pursuing a more mainstream music career. If she wanted to break through, she was going to have to produce music that was going to sell in its millions. The journey towards the mainstream had begun.

As Katy opened up, however, she began to discover a

world she hadn't known existed before. Her intensely sheltered childhood meant she had only ever met people like herself, and now that was beginning to change. 'My gospel career was going nowhere,' she told *Vanity Fair*. 'Letting go was a process. Meeting gay people, or Jewish people, and realizing that they were fine was a big part of it. Once I stopped being chaperoned, and realized I had a choice in life, I was like, "Wow, there are a lot of choices." I began to become a sponge for all that I had missed – the music, the movies. I was as curious as the cat.'

This showed some considerable determination on Katy's part: the world of showbusiness is littered with wannabes who once appeared to have a great future but failed at the first hurdle and then gave up. Now that Katy was determined to try again, the big question was, with whom? Although she'd made plenty of contacts in Nashville, none of them seemed the right person to lead her in this next step in her career – until she saw Glen Ballard, that is, and learned of his connection to Alanis Morissette. Katy first saw him on television and was determined to make contact.

The way Katy tells it, it sounds very simple, but it wasn't. 'At sixteen I was just like, "OK, well this is over. What do I do now?"' she told CBS News. 'I watched VH1 and I saw Glen Ballard. And he was talking about Alanis Morissette's *Jagged Little Pill* and I was like, "Well, that's a really good record. She speaks from my perspective. I want to make a record like that!"' First, however, she had to engineer a meeting, then she had to convince Glen she was good enough. It worked, but not without some effort on her part.

Glen was to prove the next hugely influential musician in Katy's career. Born in 1953 in Natchez, Mississippi, Glen was a musical prodigy, playing the piano from infancy, composing by the age of ten and joining local rock bands from a very young age. Early influences included Jerry Lee Lewis (who lived in the area), Al Green and, from further afield, The Beatles. A degree in English, political science and journalism at the University of Mississippi followed, and it was while he was studying that he released his one and only solo record. In the end, though, he knew he was better off working behind the scenes.

Just as Katy was to do nearly thirty years later, Glen realized that his future lay in LA, so he packed his bags and moved, finding work with Elton John's then company and composing a hit for Kiki Dee. That led to a truly spectacular career as a songwriter, although it wasn't until his association with Alanis Morissette that he broke into the public consciousness, culminating in him winning six Grammy awards and being involved in the sale of nearly 150 million records. Along with his songwriting partner, Dave Stewart, Glen has contributed to numerous films, including *Ghost* and *Hanna Montana: the Movie*.

This, then, was the man whom Katy saw as her future, and in many ways she was right. It took a certain amount of self-possession to persuade him of the fact, but at least she was fortunate enough to have a Nashville associate to set up a meeting between the two of them. 'So, I went home that night with my mom to the hotel and in the hotel room, I turn on VH1, and I saw Glen Ballard talking about Alanis Morissette,' Katy told The Star Scoop. 'I thought, you know what, I want to work with him; that's who I'm gonna work with. So the next day I came into the studio and I said, I want to work with this guy named Glen Ballard. He's like, okay, well I can pull all the strings I have and make that happen. He got me a meeting with Glen in Los Angeles, and I had my dad drive me up to LA.'

There was a huge amount at stake: Katy knew she had to get this one right – it could be an enormous opportunity if she cracked it, but she'd fall flat on her face if she failed. Katy was nothing if not determined, though – she would need to be over the next few years – so she prepared to give it her all.

'I said, Dad, stay in the car,' she continued. 'I'm just gonna go in, play a song for this guy and come back out. And I did, and I guess it went well, because I got the call the next day. So, he did develop me for a few years and then through all kinds of events.'

In actual fact, Glen was impressed from the moment Katy opened her mouth: she had the voice and, just as importantly, she had star quality. After that first meeting, Glen saw instantly that he had a real star on his hands, and was certain Katy was going to be huge, so it's perhaps surprising that in the end the breakthrough took so long.

The two recalled their first meeting in an interview on *CBS News*: 'I was a million miles away working on something else,' said Glen.

'And I walked in with my guitar,' said Katy. 'And I played him a song.'

'She played the song and it was OK, that's all I needed to know,' said Glen.

'And then he called me the next day and said, "I want to move you to Los Angeles. I want to help fulfill your dreams,"' Katy added.

Meanwhile Katy had started to encounter a new problem, one that was going to get worse as her career continued to stall: she was seen as soiled goods. It was mightily unfair, but when she made her first album, *Katy Hudson*, she was an unknown quantity with nothing to lose. Now that she had tried and failed, however, record companies would judge her on that. Jennifer Knapp had been right to voice reservations: Katy was still awfully young to be taking all of all this on board.

Katy had had time to rethink, though, and in the wake of her first meeting with Glen she reached several conclusions. For a start, her name was going to have to change. Katy Hudson was just too close to the name of Goldie Hawn's daughter, Kate Hudson, and it had started to cause confusion, something that couldn't go on if she had any intention of making her mark. Consequently, she adopted her mother's maiden name, becoming Katy Perry.

Secondly, whilst being in Nashville had been enormously helpful in terms of her musical development, it wasn't helping her career. She needed to be close to the centre of the action, and so, at the tender age of seventeen, she moved on again, setting up home in Los Angeles.

It was a gamble, however, and for some years it didn't look as if it would pay off. Despite Glen's initial enthusiasm, the success Katy desired continued to elude her, and it would be many years before she finally began to make an impact on the music world.

Meanwhile, Katy's association with Jennifer was, if not exactly at an end, then altered. Jennifer was having her own issues with the music business: while she continued to be massively successful, personal circumstances made her review where she wanted to go next. In 2004, she announced that she was taking a break from the industry, and several years after that, it emerged that she'd been in a same-sex relationship since 2002. It wasn't her lesbian relationship that made her take stock, she maintained in later interviews, but stress and burnout, and she continued to be a practising Christian. She returned to music several years later, and has since moved to Australia, where she took up Australian citizenship.

Now newly relocated in LA, Katy and Glen began working together, talking to record labels and working out a strategy for the months ahead. Whilst writing music under the aegis of her new friend, Katy was starting to learn about her adopted home town and sorting out her domestic arrangements, including getting a car, an apartment – which she shared with a Christian singer her parents approved of – and setting herself up as a girl about town. There was a faint buzz about her: Glen's success with Alanis had been such that if he said someone was the next big thing, people listened. Back home, Katy's parents continued to be supportive, even if they were a little worried about what their little girl was going to do next.

It was at around this time that Katy embarked on her first serious relationship – one of only three – with fellow singer Matt Thiessen of the group Relient K. The couple met through Glen: like Katy, Matt was a religious singer and Relient K is a Christian rock band. Matt was born in St Catharines, Ontario, on 12 August 1980, and his parents divorced when he was just six, after which Matt's mother remarried. The family moved to Bolivar, Ohio, where Matt grew up and where he met Matt Hoopes and Brian Pittman, with whom, in 1998, he founded Relient K (the band is named after Hoopes' Plymouth Relient K car). They released their first CD, *2000 A.D.D.*, in 2000 and enjoyed some success from the very start. Matt went on to write 'The One I'm Waiting For', inspired, he said, by Katy. The couple were to stay together for about two years, and the break-up when it came was amicable.

The repercussions of the relationship continued to reverberate for many a year to come. Matt, along with Katy and Glen, wound up writing a song called 'Long Shot' together, which eventually ended up on a Kelly Clarkson album. 'I dated Katy and during that time she was working on her record, and I just tagged along as a boyfriend,' Matt later recalled to azcentral.com. 'Fortunately, my musical abilities got put to work, and they let me help write. Then, six years later, Kelly Clarkson gets a leftover cut from Katy's record. I've heard that Kelly doesn't actually like the song. She feels it's a leftover from Katy, which sucks for me because she doesn't play it live and won't release it as a single. But it's all good.'

The relationship wasn't destined to last, however. Nor was success within Katy's grasp, although there were a few false dawns that seemed to herald a breakthrough.

Encouraged by Glen, Katy had signed up with Island Def Jam Recordings, and had started work on a new album. Island Def Jam was a very different set-up from Red Hill Records, however. For a start, it wasn't a Christian record company, but a mainstream one, founded in 1999 when Universal Music Group merged two of its subsidiaries, Island Records and Def Jam Recordings. At the time of Katy's brief involvement with them, it also contained the staff, roster and back catalogue of Mercury Records. The two had separate artists and musical styles, with Island – Katy's label – specializing in pop and rock, whilst Def Jam was for rap and R&B.

Island was home to some of the biggest names in the business, so this time round Katy had every reason to hope her career would fulfil its early promise. She spent the best part of a year working on songs, including 'Long Shot', for an album that was pencilled in for release in 2005, and she was hopeful that now, at last, her music would reach a wider audience. Yet again, though, Katy was about to be disappointed. This time it wasn't the album that did badly, though: the album didn't do anything at all. Island bosses started to doubt that their young charge could hack it, so Katy was dropped and no record was released. Katy was right back where she'd started. If ever she needed resolve, now was the time. This was a second kick in the teeth, and in many ways it was more personal than the last time. Previously, Katy's record company had collapsed, this time her label simply weren't interested any more.

It was a big blow. 'I was in Beverly Hills with my new Jetta, thinking that my album was about to come out, and I was so excited,' she told *Vanity Fair*. 'Then nothing happened. It was like, "Wow, my car's getting repossessed, I have no money, and I'm living on Cahuenga under the Hollywood sign."'

Katy has made light of this period of her life in later years, but in reality it must have been tough, and not just because she wasn't receiving the adulation she craved. She wasn't earning much, either, meaning she was forced to lead a very precarious hand-to-mouth lifestyle that on occasion teetered dangerously close to the edge. Her parents were in no position to help her and at times matters were really dire. Financially, things were reaching crisis stage: if something didn't happen soon, she was going to have to do something else, otherwise she wouldn't be able to feed herself. Perhaps a career in music wasn't for her after all?

To her great credit, Katy decided to stick it out. She wanted to be a musician, and if she gave up now that really would have been it. Still in her teens, with one failed record behind her and having been dropped by a major music label, Katy decided to keep going. In the end, she did what many people in her situation do: she gave herself a deadline, and if it didn't work by then she would try something else. 'I gave myself a timeline,' she explained to *Elle* magazine years later. 'I thought, OK, if I don't make it by twenty-five, I'm just going to get married and pop out some babies and do some crafts.' For now, however, she would keep going. Katy was both determined and ambitious, and she was not prepared to give up, even if it proved to be a massive struggle.

The fact that she was failing to get to where she wanted was encouraging dangerous new habits, however. Still only a teenager, she started hitting the bottle to blur the pain. 'What else was I gonna do?' she said to *Blender* magazine. 'I'd just turn into a depressed, pill-popping disaster of a housewife. It was really difficult, drinking became a problem. It got out of control until I said, OK – back to work. I know I'm speaking for someone, even if it is someone silly.'

Katy was flirting with disaster. A combination of alcohol, lack of success and not enough focus was taking its toll: she was getting drunk, waking up hungover and feeling worse than ever, until her father intervened. Her parents' own wild pasts meant they knew how to deal with this latest crisis. Until that time, Katy hadn't been entirely aware of her parents' misspent youth, but they were able to use their experiences to explain to her that it was an unwise road to take, and in the end Katy listened and backed off from the edge.

It was time to start again, although in fairness, not all the work she did with Glen was wasted. Apart from 'Long Shot', the two had also produced three other songs: 'Box',

'Diamonds' and 'Simple'. The first two of these were pasted on Katy's MySpace page as a calling card of sorts, while the third made it onto the soundtrack of the 2005 film *The Sisterhood of the Traveling Pants*. Katy and Glen remained on good terms: he still had faith in her even if he was finding it difficult to get anyone else to feel the same way.

A great deal of the work Katy was doing at this stage was for advertisements. 'She was touring and making music, but it wasn't the kind of touring she'd previously imagined. 'There was the silly string incident,' she later told online magazine Prefix. 'I was playing a concert and decided I wanted a beach theme. No particular reason, I'm just fun like that. The band entered to 'Wipe Out' and everybody was wearing their bathing suits. I should mention at this point that we were doing this show for Garnier Fructis haircare products, and they've spent like an hour and a half getting my hair just right. So I'm out there in my bathing suit with my awesome hair and I have some silly string. I don't know why I have the silly string, of course. It's just kind of fun. So I point it at the audience and try to spray them. Only instead of spraying it at the audience I had the can backward and sprayed it all over my awesome hair. Everybody thought that was pretty funny. Except maybe the hair people, I guess.'

In 2004, there was another breakthrough. This time round it was Columbia Records who spotted Katy's potential and signed her to their label. One of the giants of the American entertainment industry and part of Sony Music

Entertainment, it seemed like an ideal launch pad, and initially their collaboration was very productive as they teamed her with The Matrix, a well-respected production team with a good track record in producing female stars.

The Matrix consisted of three people: Lauren Christy, who'd had some recording success in the 1990s, her husband Graham Edwards and producer Scott Spock, all managed by Sandy Roberton. The trio had got together in 1999 and given themselves their unusual name: 'It was hard to constantly describe the three of us, so we came up with the name "The Matrix",' Lauren told Broadcast Music Inc. 'The matrix is a name for the womb, or the rock, which everything comes from.' They first wrote a song for the Australian band Jackson Mendoza, which they followed with 'This Year', which went on to Christina Aguilera's *My Kind of Christmas* in 2000. This in turn led to work with Avril Lavigne, and shortly afterwards they signed up with Columbia. By the time they linked up with Katy, they had worked with Busted, Hilary Duff, Jason Mraz, Shakira, Britney Spears and Miranda Cosgrove. Numerous awards and Grammy nominations flowed in, making them look perfect for Katy. What could possibly go wrong?

Initially, it appeared, nothing at all. Another singer, the British AKA, who released one album, *Pigeonomics*, through J-Bird Records and was briefly signed to J Records, was recruited, and work began on an album of light-hearted pop songs. *Blender* called Katy the 'next big thing' and Katy herself thought that at long last she was on her way. She made jokes about losing her credibility, but far worse was the fact that until now she'd been going nowhere: finally things seemed to be happening.

Meanwhile Katy's body was developing, too, and she was becoming a very shapely woman – a fact she was acutely aware of. Just as Katy was starting to find her musical style, so she began experimenting in other ways. Her appearance was still of paramount importance to her, but now she'd gone beyond an addiction to black nail varnish and became attracted to the vintage look she eventually made her own. There was no plan behind it, it just happened. She'd started sporting a 1950s appearance back in the Santa Barbara days, and now it became part of her look.

Whilst Katy was growing into her figure, it was a struggle at times. 'I was shaped like a square at one time. I was!' she told *Elle* magazine. 'I'm generally around 130 pounds, which is totally fine for me. But when I was a kid, I was the same height and weighed more like 145. And I had enormous boobs that I didn't know what to do with, so I wore minimizers, which were not cute. Those thick-ass straps! I got made fun of for the over-the-shoulder boulder holder . . . and all I wanted was to look like Kate Moss. Little did I know . . . that these things would come in handy someday.'

Those boobs were beginning to come in handy already. Katy was still having to wait for a breakthrough, but she was finally starting to get noticed, and her appearance obviously had something to do with it. No one denied her talent or fine voice, but in an industry where being noticed is crucial, a signature look certainly helps. Katy was cute and retro, with a touch of Minnie Mouse about her. She was pretty enough to attract men, but not so beautiful as to frighten women. She was just about getting it right.

Another thing that was appealing about Katy was that she's a girly girl. She wasn't embarrassed about it and was sweetly engaging when it came to 'fessing up to the preoccupations of a young woman. 'I love shopping, like vintage shopping,' she told The Star Scoop in 2008. 'Not just going to a store, picking up clothes with labels or whatever. I love hunting, going to estate sales, and going to thrift stores, look for antiques. My mom used to be an antique dealer in her younger years, and I'm thinking maybe I got that obsession as well. I like to blog as well. I did a little bit of blogging as of lately. Surfing the World Wide Web.'

It was those early years when she didn't have any money that prompted her to develop her appearance in the way she did. With her car getting repossessed and her cheques bouncing, there wasn't much money left over to spend on designer clobber, so Katy was forced to find her clothes as cheaply as she could, and that meant vintage.

Meanwhile, work continued on the new album. Katy was still planning a project with Glen, but in the meantime things were going well with The Matrix and it seemed like Katy's dream was finally about to come true. Until – it didn't. Behind the scenes, the powers that be were getting worried. They were beginning to disagree with Katy about where the project should be going and there were rumours that they thought her haircut was too similar to Ashlee Simpson's – a big sensation at the time – all of which meant they were getting cold feet. And so, with 80 per cent of the album already recorded, Katy was dropped yet again.

This time it really was nearly too much for Katy. She was shattered. Not only was it really damaging for her image, it shook her confidence to the core. 'To have a whole album recorded, and never have it come out,' she told *Rolling Stone*, and although by the time she gave this interview she had become hugely successful, the shock was still evident. 'But I really believe it's part of my destiny. Or the plan. Or whatever.' At the time, it seemed as if that really was that.

Plenty of other people couldn't believe it either. 'That was a shame,' said Glen Ballard with some understatement. 'They couldn't even decide on a single. It just fell apart.' It was inexplicable. To have invested so much time and energy, only to dump the project at the last minute, didn't just betray a lack of forethought: no one seemed to have any idea what they should do with Katy. Of course, had they but known it, they were dropping someone who was to become one of the biggest success stories of the decade, although that certainly wasn't evident at the time.

Perhaps it's knockbacks like these that contributed to Katy's success. Much later, Katy was able to see it as a good move. If it had gone ahead, she might have been launched in a very different way and never have achieved the success she has found today. In the end she was able to put a good spin on it: 'Thank God that didn't come out, you know?' she said of the work she did with The Matrix. 'I had this kind of quirky, unique perspective, and they had a very mainstream-pop perspective, which was really cool, too, but I wasn't used to it. We made a record that sonically sounds brilliant but doesn't say much, even though there's a few songs I still love. My own stuff is very heart-on-my-sleeve.'

At the time things seemed more desperate than ever. Katy had been dropped no less than three times and, with the best will in the world, that's hardly a ringing endorsement for finding a new record label. There were also a number of other issues that were bringing her down, such as lack of money, no way of earning a living and no future in an industry she loved. If ever anyone's resolve was being tested, it was Katy's, and it must have taken a will of iron not to let events destroy her self-confidence.

Totally broke and confronting the possibility that it probably wasn't going to happen, she was forced to take a job in A&R at Taxi Music, a small record label based outside LA. 'That was the most depressing moment of my hustle,' she told the *Guardian*. 'I was sitting there in a cubicle, with 25 other trying-to-make-it-some-failed artists in a box listening to the worst music you've ever heard in your entire life. Having no money, writing bad cheques, renting a car after two cars had been repossessed, trying to give people constructive criticism and hope, when really I wanted to jump out of the building or cut my ears off and say, "I can't help you! I can't catch a break. What am I gonna say to you? And you sing off tune." '

These comments, trivial as they might seem, have caused a great deal of anger in some quarters from people who haven't been as fortunate as Katy eventually became. Internet forums were established on the back of what she said, with many people furious that she'd dared to imply that all the music she listened to at Taxi wasn't up to scratch. On the Just Plain Folks Music Organisation message boards, a long thread started entitled 'Katy Perry insult to Taxi and it's [sic] members' and it was apparent those members were not happy with what they heard.

'Katy Perry talked about her background as a song critiquer for Taxi and made an insulting remark about the quality of the songs and seemingly demeaned Taxi as well,' snapped pomeranj. 'It smacked of elitism and angered me greatly.'

Noel Downs was more sympathetic (and self-deprecating.) 'She's right there are a lot of truly bad songs out there . . . I've written a number of them myself . . . Just show [sic] how good a job taxi does . . . too bad that it comes across like a nasty poke . . .'

Hummingbird, however, was less sympathetic. 'Obviously she is not cut out to be a mentor to aspiring songwriters, artists and composers. That takes tremendous patience, the ability to teach on the fly, in-depth knowledge, and the ability to be honest while also being encouraging.'

And so it went on. The fact that a throwaway remark

could prompt such debate is a sign of how successful Katy's become, though, and if it was a little tactless, well, Katy had paid her dues. Back then, however, the situation was beginning to seem hopeless. Just what was she going to have to do to find fame?

A New Dawn

For a while it seemed as if it was all over. Katy was stuck in a dead-end job she hated, supplementing her income by borrowing from her parents and wondering where it all went so badly wrong. Dumped by three record labels, her early dreams of stardom had completely melted and Katy was beginning to think she should give it all up and start having babies instead. She had seen up close how competitive the music world could be and, not previously prone to self-doubt, she was now riven with it. Not only was it depressing, it was humiliating to have been dumped so often when the future had once looked so bright. 'It turned into a situation where, for years, I was telling my friends that I was going to have a record out – like, I had the CD art and everything – and then it wouldn't happen,' she said. 'They stopped believing in me. I was pretty much a joke.'

But not everyone had stopped believing in her. Glen Ballard was still convinced that one day she was going to be a major star, and it was through him that Katy ended up working with the Christian band P.O.D., appearing in their video and singing on the track 'Goodbye For Now', which appeared on their album *Testify*. It might not have had the high profile she hankered after, but it kept her in practice, in the business, and it added to the bank of knowledge she was building up. It was also the first single she appeared on before promoting her own major release a couple of years later. Even then, at her lowest ebb and when it seemed her career was going nowhere, Katy's presence added value. Her star quality is there if you look hard enough. Presciently, Andree Farias of Christianity Today International, commented that it added 'to the pop appeal of the song'. It seemed that some people could see that Katy had the makings of a major pop star, even if the record companies were being a little slow on the uptake.

Crucially it gave Katy a little taste of success, albeit at one remove. 'Goodbye For Now' was played a great deal on the radio and featured in the promotional videos for the film *The Chronicles of Narnia: the Lion, the Witch and the Wardrobe*. The lyrics themselves related very much to Katy's own Christian beliefs and yet they segued into her nascent pop career, too.

'It's more of a laid-back track, it's more of a vibe track, it's definitely not the heavy side of P.O.D., but lyrically it's a hopeful song,' said singer Sonny Sandoval to MTV. 'We know with just dealing with the people around us and just coming across so many people that there are a lot of people struggling out there. And being that positive influence that we like to have in our music, we are just trying to encourage people. No matter how bad today is, tomorrow has a bright promise and a bright future. There's a lyric that says, "If joy really comes in the morning time/Then

I'm going to sit back and wait until the next sunrise." And in our faith, we believe that joy does come in the morning time, so just hold on and hang out and tomorrow is a whole different day.'

Katy also made an appearance on Carbon Leaf's video for 'Learn To Fly' as the two acts shared the same management team. By this time, Katy was starting to approach her career from a different angle to see if she had what it takes to be an actress on the silver screen rather than a singer. At least it kept her busy and stopped her from falling into despair.

Carbon Leaf wasn't an obvious association for Katy, as the five-piece rock band from Richmond, Virginia, came from a Celtic/Bluegrass music background, although by the time Katy met them they'd gone more mainstream. Like Katy, though, they'd had to struggle to make it and their early work was released on their own label, Constant Ivy Music. Several years on, of course, they were forced to sit back and watch as the young actress from the video leapfrogged them in the hall of fame, becoming better known than they would ever be. Carbon Leaf singer Barry Privett was generous about it: 'It's funny,' he said when asked about Katy making it big. 'We shared the same management company at the time. We made that video a year or two before her record. It was interesting to experience that and see her blow up. Good for her, right?'

Katy's brief change of tack also led to an appearance on the Gym Class Heroes' video for 'Cupid's Chokehold', playing the love interest of the lead singer, Travis McCoy, a role that would eventually spill over into real life . . .

Whilst Katy's star quality was undeniable, her look was still evolving. Now a mature woman, as opposed to the fresh-faced teen she'd been when she'd started out, she had blossomed into a beauty. Her looks were certainly never going to stand in the way of her success, and for a while they helped to earn her keep. By 2007, Katy had appeared in advertisements for Too Faced Cosmetics, which helped prove that she was photogenic, if nothing else. Too Faced got an additional boost when Katy became famous and public interest in her past rocketed, as they got to reap the benefits of using her in their advertising campaign a second time around.

Despite her acting appearances, most people thought she'd blown it musically: 'I had someone say to me that "Psst, you should probably go home, because you're never gonna get signed again",' Katy told CBS News. '"You're pretty much damaged goods. And you should be in the defect aisle at [American store chain] Ross." And I'm twenty at that point. I'm like, "I'm defected goods already?"' It was a tough lesson in how bitchy showbusiness people can be.

Fortunately, Glen was still there for her. 'I encouraged Katy to not so much rebel against anything she's been through, but to actually use it toward defining who she really was as a person,' he said. That meant calling on all her reserves of self-belief and ambition, and forcing herself to carry on when everything seemed hopeless — not an easy thing to do. Matters were getting desperate, not least because she wasn't earning anything like enough money to keep herself: 'I'd write a check for my rent and next to it, I'd write, "Please, God, please,"' Katy confessed afterwards. 'But I didn't jump off the Hollywood sign. Everything always works out for the best.'

It was now, just as it seemed she was never going to get anywhere, that Katy finally had what would turn out to be her major break, proving that all those years spent paying her dues hadn't been wasted.

Jason Flom is one of the most successful and respected executives in the American music industry. The son of an equally successful Manhattan lawyer, Jason grew up in New York, played in his own band as a teenager and then shocked everyone by going into the music business rather than attending college and following in his father's footsteps by becoming a lawyer. It was to prove a resoundingly right decision. In 1979 he joined Atlantic Records, where he came to the attention of Atlantic's founder Ahmet Ertegun; shortly afterwards he moved to the A&R department where he worked with Twisted Sister and Skid Row, and it was clear from the outset that he was an extremely talented man who totally understood the music scene.

A meteoric career ensued as Jason worked with some of the most successful artists of the day, among them Jewel, Hootie & the Blowfish, Collective Soul, Tori Amos and Stone Temple Pilots, not to mention discovering Kid Rock. He founded Lava Records, an imprint of Atlantic, and went on to sell his share of Lava to Warner Music,

Atlantic's parent company, for $50 million. In 2005, he became CEO of Virgin Records, and when it became part of Capitol, he became CEO of that company, too. A noted philanthropist who's worked with various charitable organizations, including Families Against Mandatory Minimums, the Legal Action Center and the Drug Policy Alliance, he returned to Lava Records in 2009, and at the time of writing his most recent discovery is Jessie J.

This, then, was the man who was to rescue Katy from oblivion and kick-start one of the most successful pop careers of modern times. As Katy tells it, in her trademark jokey style, it pretty much happened overnight, when she was working at the job she'd grown to hate so much. 'I was sitting in a cube, listening to all this horrible music people had sent in and critiquing it, because I was supposed to be helping them get ahead in the music industry,' she told *Billboard* magazine. 'Then Jason Flom called me. That day I went out for coffee and never went back.'

In actual fact, of course, it was rather more complicated than that, and there were various stories flying about in the aftermath of her success as to who really did what. There's no doubting that Jason Flom was the real hero of the hour, though. Some time after Katy first found success, Jason wrote a letter to Bob Lefsetz, who writes a music industry newsletter, and this was leaked on the internet, providing a fascinating insider's view on how it all came about. In it, Flom writes that Katy 'impressed me from the first moment with her charisma and her drive and then I heard her music and I was sold'.

Jason was the man who changed Katy's life, but he had help in the form of Angelica Cob-Baehler, Virgin's head of publicity. When Katy came to their attention, the timing was perfect. Jason had started at Virgin in October 2005, at a time when the company had been unable to break a really successful act in the United States for some years. This became Jason's priority. After some fairly ruthless trimming of the existing Virgin list, he concentrated his attention on the best of what was left. The strategy worked: existing Virgin acts began to perform well and new performers started to break through.

By now, Jason was working with the likes of Lenny Kravitz, Coldplay and the Rolling Stones, and it was on the strength of that success that he decided to break a new international act. He needed someone who would appeal to men and women alike, who had star quality, who had the talent and personality to carry off an international career and who wouldn't succumb to the downside of fame as soon as he or she got there. It's a testament to Jason's reputation as an industry hotshot that he chose Katy.

Katy, meanwhile, was still with Columbia, although rumours were rife that she was about to be dropped, yet again. While this would have put many people off her – she would have been signed to four record labels in seven years, which must be approaching a record – Jason not only saw her potential, he had the *cojones* to back up his hunch.

Jeff Kempler was the executive vice president of Virgin Records at the time Katy was signed, and he gave a lengthy account of the behind-the-scenes negotiations to Hit-Quarters. They were all taking a leap of faith, given Katy's recent track record, albeit one that was to pay off in spectacular style. By this time the main problem seemed to be not whether or not she was talented, but whether they'd be able to find the right material for her. In the end, of course, they did.

'In the summer or fall of 2006, while Jason, Lee, and I and a few other senior Virgin executives were en route to an iTunes visit in Cupertino, Jason started hyping us on a girl that he believed could be that [international break-through] act – Katy Perry,' Kempler told HitQuarters. 'He said she was still signed to Columbia, but heard she was being dropped and proceeded to risk all of our hearing by playing us the records Katy had made for Columbia at top volume while he sang along to pretty much every line, especially "Thinking Of You" and "Waking Up In Vegas". Frankly, despite Jason's enthusiasm, reactions in the car were mixed, and Jason's only concession to the peanut gallery was that he felt Katy needed at least one, if not two, more obvious radio smashes. We discussed that Katy had been dropped by Island before Columbia, and he reminded us that he had signed Kid Rock after Rock was dropped by Jive "and that worked out pretty well".'

Indeed it had, and the clout it had given Jason was the only way he was able to persuade everyone else to sign Katy. Both money and reputation were at risk here; no one wanted a high-profile failure. As for Katy, if matters didn't turn out well for her this time, she'd almost certainly had it, so it was crucial that everyone got the details right. This time, however, the people who really mattered were determined to see her succeed.

'Towards the end of 2006, we had picked up that Katy's exit from Columbia (and the Glen Ballard JV through which she was signed) was not going smoothly,' Kempler continued. 'However, Angelica Cob-Baehler, our head of publicity (who would later become and still is a key leader at EMI on all things Katy Perry), just would not let it go. She had worked with Katy at Columbia and was constantly in Jason's and my ear that we absolutely had to sign this girl, which Jason wanted to do – assuming deals could be worked out with Ballard and Columbia. So Katy was a regular topic of conversation over the 2006/07 winter holidays and into early 2007. At some point in or around January, Jason told me he was dead set that we sign Katy. So in tandem with our head of business affairs, Phil Wild, we re-opened direct conversations with Ballard and Katy's representatives and created a business structure that would facilitate Katy signing to Virgin, and bringing along her existing masters, with Columbia and Ballard's blessing.'

Behind the corporate jargon, the message was clear: after one of the longest apprenticeships in pop history, Katy was on her way, signing to a newly created company called Capitol Music Group, a merger between Capitol and Virgin. There were some complex negotiations to be made, given the extent of the work that Katy had done with Columbia, and as part of the deal, her new record label took over the rights to much of the work she'd already done, which would feature on her debut album, *One of the Boys*.

Now, for the first time, Katy was with people who seemed to know what to do with her, and fortunately for her, they were also aware of the problems as well as the opportunities. Although they were happy to use much of the material she'd already recorded, they didn't have that all-important number with a certain edge. The music was 'very strong but lacking an undeniable smash or two that would work both on US pop radio and internationally', according to Jason. He was therefore extremely keen to encourage a collaboration between Katy and the song-writer Dr Luke, which would result in one of the biggest hit singles of recent years.

Dr Luke (née Lukasz Gottwald) was another of the cast that assembled around Katy back then, and he was to play a key role in her future success. Born on 26 September 1973 in Rhode Island to an architect father and interior designer mother of American–Polish heritage, he spent much of his childhood in New York and learned to play the guitar – he'd wanted to be a drummer, but his parents wouldn't allow a drum kit in the house – before being expelled from various schools for drug-related offences.

Even so, he made it to the Manhattan School of Music, where he studied for two years. This gave him something in common with Katy, who'd also been trained in various different musical styles, although Dr Luke himself is fairly ambivalent about his formal training, telling *American Song-writer*, 'It's been very important at times, but it may have also been a hindrance. There's something really pure about people who don't know that stuff. They just feel it and go with it. But then there's certain times when people hit a dead end and don't know how to get out of it. That's when the training comes in – for the music problem-solving. When I started studying music, you learn about voice leading and Bach chorales and there are all these rules and this and that. You start understanding things and then it becomes a go-to to do things that way. I've seen other people become incredible players but not incredible composers because of that. It can be a problem.'

But not for him. Dr Luke made it to the *Saturday Night Live* band as lead guitarist, where he stayed for ten years from 1997 to 2007. *Saturday Night Live* is a major prime-time US television programme and the exposure and experience proved invaluable. It was during this time that Luke began DJing in New York, writing jingles and ads and becoming involved in the hip-hop scene. He then made the acquaintance of Max Martin, who was hugely influential in 1990s pop music. The Swedish-born songwriter was responsible for what could be seen as a precursor to Katy's hits – 'Baby, One More Time' by Britney Spears – as well as another massive hit, 'I Want It That Way' by the Backstreet Boys. Eventually the two songwriters started collaborating.

'We were friends for a long time before we started working,' Max told *Billboard* magazine. 'I came to New York and just wanted to write something, so I called him up, because I knew he had a studio in his basement. We started working, and I instantly knew, because his instincts are really, how do you say it? He wants it to be effective. I was struck by that. "No, no, that's too long. Get to the point!" And I'm known for that. But he took it even further, and I really liked that.'

Around 2004, Dr Luke became heavily involved in writing and producing music, setting up two production companies and working with the likes of Kelly Clarkson, for whom he wrote the huge breakthrough hit, 'Since U Been Gone', which was the first of many collaborations with Max Martin. 'I met him when I was DJing,' Dr Luke recalled to *American Songwriter* years later. 'One day he called me when he was in town and asked me if he could use my studio. I had this really crappy studio in my basement of my duplex apartment. We think it was the first song we wrote together. He taught me to think bigger, to strive for more. And we still work together to this day. Clive Davis [Grammy-award-winning record producer] told me that "Since U Been Gone" would be on the radio in April. It came out in October. I remember counting the months. I remember thinking he was crazy, that he was out of his mind. But he was right. Never doubt Clive Davis.'

Strangely enough Kelly, an *American Idol* winner, had, like Katy, had problems establishing herself initially, only managing to break through with Dr Luke's help. Without that hit she would be yet another music industry statistic, a talent who'd flowered briefly and then disappeared. Such was Dr Luke's influence that she had a complete career turnaround with that song, and he acquired the name

Dr Luke as a result of that recording. He became the man of the moment and went on to collaborate with Pink, Avril Lavigne and the Sugababes, amongst others. Now it was Dr Luke, along with Jason Flom and assorted others, who was to change Katy's life.

The pace Dr Luke set himself, and the hours and hard work he put in, were to set the template for the way he worked with artists and collaborators from then on. 'We'd work in the studio until five in the morning, then wake up and get at it again,' says Ke$ha, another Dr Luke success story. 'I was really broke and he'd let me crash on a mattress in his spare bedroom. We did yoga and would go hiking and swimming together; he gave me advice about boys.' Work, however, dominated. As one of the most successful songwriters of his generation, Dr Luke put the hours in, so much so that when asked about his personal life, he pretended not to know what the phrase meant.

What was the secret of Dr Luke's success? For a young man, he certainly knew what young girls wanted to listen to, something he would good-naturedly acknowledge in interviews. He had three sisters, he would tell everyone, and thus instinctively knew what girls liked.

'Apparently my taste is that of a thirteen-year-old girl,' he told *Billboard* magazine. 'Not really. But my taste is commercial. Listen, there's been times in my life like the two years that I only listened to jazz, and probably nothing after 1966. When I went to the Manhattan School of Music, the library didn't have anything after 1966. In order to get good at that, I had to tunnel-vision and focus on that. But sometimes when I talk to those kinds of people, they're like, "What is it like making this simple music?" They look down on it. And I'm like, "No, you don't get it. I actually like this. I don't see a difference between brilliance in one and the other." There's no compromise to me in what I'm doing. I'm trying to make songs that I love and make them feel a certain way and go to certain places. It just so happens that a lot of thirteen-year-old girls like that.'

Or perhaps he had just never grown up. On making a good pop song, he told CBS News, 'The hardest thing, and the most difficult thing, is to do the most simple thing. Because that means that you've had to weed out every other option. I kind of feel like that about a good pop song, too. When it's right, it's perfect, you know?'

He had certainly happened on a remarkably successful formula. 'A Dr Luke song reliably involves tension-building verses followed by a soaring, strap-yourself-in chorus (a poppified take on the old grunge approach); no end of bleep-blorp synthesizing (both instrumental and vocal) borrowed gleefully from eighties electro-pop; and an unapologetic, don't-even-think-you-won't-be-humming-this-all-summer hook,' according to *New York* magazine.

'He's successfully cracked the secret to what once seemed like a musical oxymoron: the aggressively sunny song that melds "the veneer of rock and the sheen of pop", in the words of Sean Fennessey, a critic for *Spin* and the website Village Voice.' In many ways he was the natural successor to Phil Spector, creator of the famous wall-of-sound style of music that dominated the 1960s, and who's now serving a life sentence for murder.

Katy and Dr Luke hit it off right away: they were going to have to, given how closely they'd be working together. They had a fair bit in common, though. As well as both having elements of the musical prodigy about them when they were young, both had trained in more formal musical styles. They were also both extremely hardworking, determined and prepared to keep working away until they finally produced the right sound. As well as getting on, they perfectly complemented one another. Dr Luke is a behind-the-scenes man – recent invitations to take part in reality television shows have been turned down flat – whereas Katy is very much a front-of-stage star. So while Dr Luke would create the circumstances, Katy would go out and knock everyone's socks off. She was able to trust him because, on a personal level, they didn't want the same things.

'It's different every time, depending on the artists and the genre and the medium,' Dr Luke told *American Song-writer* about the composing process. 'The one consistent thing is I keep going until it's right. I don't give up, and I make sure to keep my standards high. It helps to collaborate with other people because then if everyone thinks the song is good, it's more likely that it really is.' As for whether it would be a hit: 'Most of the time, that's what people seem to want from me. But it's not just "Do you want a hit?" More importantly, it has to be something we – the artist and I – like. If you go in just wanting a hit song, it's not going to happen that way. You have to first be committed to making music you like.'

This, then, was the man to whom Katy's future was to be entrusted, and the choice couldn't have been a better one. With a vast amount of experience behind him, especially of working with artists who'd had problems breaking through, Dr Luke was exactly the person to turn to. Importantly, he wasn't under any illusions about the business and how difficult it could be. Everything had to come together: nothing could be left to chance. As well as having enough experience to insist on having his own way, Dr Luke had clout within the industry. With such a successful body of work behind him, he simply wouldn't allow a project he was involved with to fail: that would look as bad from his point of view as it would from the artist's.

Dr Luke had professionalism, experience, determination and a serious work ethic and, crucially, he knew that nothing could be left to chance. 'A hit song is the right song, with the right artist, at the right time,' he told *New York* magazine. 'It's a million things going right, and any one thing can derail it. So I want to make sure the right decisions are being made – or, more important, that the wrong decisions aren't being made.'

This was what Katy needed now. Although her record company was fully behind her, she'd had enough of being passed around record labels and music executives, with no one knowing quite what to do with her. Now finally she seemed to have ended up with a committed record label, a workaholic songwriter and a producer who was generally considered to be one of the best in the business – and all of them were looking out for her. All she needed was the right song, the right album and the right launch pad. It seemed like she had been waiting for this moment for almost her entire adult life. Just how hard was it really going to be?

Changing Direction

Katy was beginning to realize that this time it was finally going to happen. She had some of the most important and experienced people in the music business batting for her and, as the project progressed, there were no hitches. Everyone was aware of the importance of getting the first single right, and that was the priority now.

Although Dr Luke was working on the song that eventually made her name, another single became her first release. The search was also on for a unique selling point, a USP, since looks, talent and charisma were not deemed to be enough. It's no coincidence, therefore, that both of her first two singles refer to homosexuality in their titles – something for which Katy would go on to receive a lot of stick from all directions. It was a daring move as Katy was being marketed at middle America, and middle America likes its teen songstresses (even though Katy wasn't actually a teen any more) to sing about boys, not girls. However, the record label wanted her to stand out, and this was one way to do it.

What the record company knew at this stage, but the public did not, was that this was totally at odds with Katy's earlier life and career as a Christian musician who was utterly devoted to her religion, and that, when the news came out, the contrast between Katy's past and present would provide a remarkably good story. If anyone was cynical enough to think about the effect that evangelical groups protesting would have on publicity, then no one actually said as much, even though that's exactly what happened. You only need to look at Madonna to see how bringing religion into the frame can make an artist dance all the way to the bank, and although Katy didn't use religious iconography, like Madonna, her background would still play its part. If it was a risk, then it was one worth taking. Middle America was just going to have to be shocked.

In truth, of course, given that Katy is not and never has been a lesbian, has only had three serious relationships – all with men – in her entire life and married the third, has never been into drugs and drinks only sparingly, it's easy to see that the difference between the Katy of yesterday and today is not that great. For all the controversy she was about to stir up, Katy is one of the cleanest living pop stars of her generation. However, the great record-buying public didn't need to know any of that just yet.

Chris Anokute, who went on to have a senior role at Universal Motown, was working at Virgin/Capitol at the time and was part of the team that launched Katy. He remembers the way it came about in an interview with Hit-Quarters. 'Jason was then talking to Dr Luke in a meeting and played him Katy Perry,' he recalled. 'He'd worked with Katy at Columbia but he'd never finished what he'd started – I guess because she wasn't a priority at Columbia. Jason convinced Dr Luke to go back into the studio with

Katy. They cut "I Kissed A Girl", "Hot N Cold" and she wrote two new songs with Greg Wells, "Ur So Gay" and "Mannequin". We probably ended up with five new songs for the record and then we picked the six best songs from the record that was on Columbia.

'We put out "Ur So Gay" as a single as a kind of intro-duction because we thought we'd have to build her story all over again. It was kind of a novelty song. We never had plans to go to radio – we just wanted to put it out online and see what the attraction was. We shot a low-budget video and the response was great. We didn't expect to sell 50,000 EPs and we sure didn't – we sold only a few thou-sand. In my opinion it did well in terms of building a press story, but because people didn't run to iTunes to buy the EP some executives in the company started backpedalling.'

So it was to be Greg Wells, and not Dr Luke, who was responsible for Katy's first official release. Greg, like Katy and Dr Luke, was both a musical prodigy and classically trained. He was born in 1969 and grew up in Peterbor-ough, Ontario, where, by the age of three, he was already playing the piano and drums; his mother and grandmother were his early teachers until he moved on to the Royal Conservatory of Music in Toronto.

'I popped out obsessed with rhythms in particular,' Greg later told HitQuarters. 'According to a family friend who's a percussion teacher, I was playing rhythms on my crib at six months. Whether that's accurate or not, I was freakishly bent towards music. I probably would have wound up professionally in music. My mum would help me read music, but my grandmother was never pushing me, she just played it by ear. So it was a thing that was happening anyway, which they tried to corral, to mould and shape a little bit.'

Childhood illness – bone disease – meant he spent his teens in a wheelchair, but this didn't stop him from mastering guitar, bass and percussion. He was a member of numerous bands, experimenting with vastly different musical styles, until he finally ended up on a music programme at the Humber College in Toronto.

His first work on a record label was with Rockland Records, but shortly afterwards he moved to LA. He then spent two years on the road with k.d. Lang's band on her Ingénue tour, which really boosted his career. 'I learned so much working with k.d., and she's still a friend of mine,' Greg told HitQuarters. 'This is a long time ago – '92–'94 – but she really took me under her wing. She had a huge record on that tour, and she won Grammys – we did three nights at the Albert Hall, three nights at Radio City Music Hall in New York. It was fantastic for me, and taught me a lot while watching a brilliant artist tour her way to a platinum record and a Grammy for best female vocal.' He was going to put those lessons to good use.

After the tour, Greg linked up with Carole King and Mark Hudson to pen the song 'The Reason', which became a massive hit for Celine Dion, then he went on to become a producer on I.R.S. Records, at the behest of Miles Copeland. Greg was well and truly on his way.

By the time he came to work with Katy, Greg had worked

with some of the biggest names in the business, including Rufus Wainwright, Mika, Pink, Jamie Cullen, OneRepublic and Deftones. And like everyone else involved with Katy's career at this stage, he was a perfectionist. 'Well, it's a lot of work – a lot of effort, a lot of focus and concentration,' he told HitQuarters. 'It's never easy. The enjoyment is at the end when you get it to where it's as it should sound, and there's a feeling of, "Ah, listen to that, finally!" But getting it there is hard. It's hard to make a good record. Real music is a live thing where you can see them doing it, not just hear it. There's an imagery from them going to the audience. You take away all those elements and you're only left with the audio coming from the speakers, and it is very unforgiving. I think that's why there's so many bad records made, as all those things that can help you through the musical experience are all gone. The speakers are merciless, and it takes a lot of effort to get the stuff coming through the speakers to move you in the way that a live experience can move you.'

With this pedigree and level of dedication, the record company wasn't taking any risks. Absolutely everyone involved was at the top of their game: experienced, determined and dedicated to making Katy a star. And so, finally, it was time to test the product, if that doesn't sound too cynical.

'Ur So Gay', Katy's first single, co-written and produced by Greg Wells, was released on 20 November 2007, as, in her own words, a 'soft hello'. It was her first ever major release and it was the culmination of an extremely long wait. Originally, the label had wanted Katy to put out a cover of another less risky song – toying with the idea of covering a hit by Queen, the band fronted by her great hero Freddie Mercury – but in the end 'Ur So Gay' was deemed more suitable. The song certainly took no prisoners.

It wasn't, perhaps, the greatest pop song ever (or even anywhere near), but it was a start. Katy had succeeded in grabbing the music industry's attention and announcing her arrival on the scene.

'It wasn't meant to be a big single or show what the album is going to be all about,' Katy told Prefix a couple of months later. 'That was for my internet bloggers, so I'm not coming out of nowhere. "Ur So Gay" was meant to be an introduction and a background. The album will have a lot of the same characteristics, though. There will be lots of storytelling, because lyrics are important to me. There are a few songs that will make you cry, but there are others to make you dance and sing. Every song is on the album for a specific reason.'

Of course, the song itself wasn't actually about homosexuality. It was the lashing out of a young woman at the end of a relationship, a canny choice given that the vast majority of Katy's fan base would almost certainly be young girls who could empathize with the song's lyrics. However, that wasn't what the pro- or anti-gay lobby took on board, and Katy was accused of promoting both homosexuality and homophobia – not for the last time either – while she confessed that the song referred to an ex (given that she only had two exes at that stage, neither could have been delighted.)

There was one small issue that had been overlooked, however: using the term 'gay' as a form of abuse, as in, 'you're so lame'. No one was very happy about that and, in retrospect, it might not have been the best decision, but everyone involved needed publicity, and being controversial certainly made the single – and Katy – stand out.

Katy herself played down any controversy. 'Every time I play that song, everybody has come back laughing,' she said. 'I'm not the type of person who walks around calling everything gay. That song is about a specific guy that I used to date and specific issues that he had. The song is about my ex wearing guyliner and taking emo [emotional] pictures of himself in the bathroom mirror. The listeners have to read the context of the song and decide for themselves.' 'Emo', of course, can be seen as a term of abuse or praise, depending on your perspective.

Was anyone who was actually gay offended? Katy was asked by *Beatweek Magazine*. 'I haven't gotten that, actually, because, you know, you listen to the song and you have to hear the whole song to realize the story,' she replied. 'I mean, there's so many songs you could just take out bits and pieces of one song and get really offended by it. Because, you know, a lot of girls, they come up to me and they say, "Oh my god, thank you so much for writing that. Here's a picture of my ex-boyfriend in clothes. You wrote this song about him. Thank you."'

The song was not a massive hit, but it did have its

admirers. 'I know the lyrics to Katy Perry's "Ur So Gay" are eighteen different kinds of wrong – the opening line about what she'd like her wayward beau to do with his H&M scarf is not for the faint of heart, nor is it entirely safe for work – but I can't stop playing this jaunty little ditty on repeat (despite its misspelled title),' wrote Michael Slezak on PopWatch. 'I don't care that there's almost no chance corporate radio will embrace a song that includes the lines: "I can't believe I fell in love/With someone who wears full make up." I am out and a proud fan of "Ur So Gay".'

He was right: it was a slightly surprising choice for mega-conservative middle America. But for that very reason it was getting attention. Sean Daly on tampabay.com enjoyed it, too: 'The boyfriend-skewering "Ur So Gay" isn't homophobic, but it does pummel straight guys who can't handle her edge,' he wrote. Not everyone agreed, though: ugo.com said it was 'catchphrase-homophobia' while Allmusic saw it as 'gaybashing'.

Indeed, the homophobia tag cropped up pretty regularly. 'It's official,' said MSNBC's Tony Sclafani, 'it's cool to make fun of gay people again.'

Gay rights campaigner Peter Tatchell didn't like it either. '[The lyrics] can be read as implicitly demeaning gay people,' he said. 'I am sure Katy would get a critical reception if she expressed comparable sentiments in a song called "Ur so black, Jewish or disabled".'

Katy found herself increasingly defensive about the charges of homophobia, which is ironic in light of what was to come next. 'The fact of the matter is that we live in a very metrosexual world,' she told *The Times*. 'You know, a girl might walk into a bar, meet a boy, and discover he's more manicured than she is. And they can't figure it out. Is he wearing foundation and a bit of bronzer? But he's buying me drinks at the same time! It's meant to be funny. I'm not saying you're so gay, you're so lame. I'm saying, you're so gay, but I don't understand it because you don't like boys!'

Still the criticism mounted. Whichever way you look at it, this song uses the word 'gay' in a negative context, and Katy was getting blamed for things she hadn't actually meant. She was finally getting noticed, but not necessarily for the right reasons. Was her pop career, so long in getting off the ground, going to stall just as it finally went out on the road? Was all this work once more going to be for nothing? Yet again, it looked as if it might all go horribly wrong.

Even Prefix, which ran a lot of sympathetic interviews with her as her career began to take off, published a very hostile review. 'On the strength of her snarky debut song, Katy Perry has been called by many one of music's next big things,' it snapped. 'So it seems she would be heading right to the top of the charts — except, of course, for the fact that "Ur So Gay", the song that she hopes will take her there, isn't so much a funny kiss-off as a juvenile bout of name-calling that borders on being offensive. "Ur So Gay" is Perry's dirty-laundry list about an ex-boyfriend.

Perry's litany of complaints is cute, but lumping all of his flaws under the umbrella of "gay" isn't especially humorous, even with Perez in her corner. If Perry were truly talented, her sense of humor would be more refined than a high school football player's. Compared with Liz Phair's acidic touch or Jill Sobule's sly witticisms, Perry calling her boyfriend gay is pedestrian.' The online magazine didn't go so far as to suggest that Perry wasn't truly talented, however, as they called the rest of the EP 'spot on'.

This was not what Katy had been expecting. 'It's not a negative connotation,' she said on another occasion, but the fact of the matter is that this boy should've been gay. I totally understand how it could be misconstrued or whatever. The video we did a while ago on a budget of little to nothing, it paints that same picture. Everyone played with that Ken Doll and they were changing his outfits.'

Katy was subjected to quite a grilling by The New Gay website, and she managed to hold her own. 'I write for a gay blog, and I thought you should know that "Ur So Gay" pissed off a lot of our readers,' her interrogator began.

'That's unfortunate,' said Katy, keeping her cool. 'It's not what I came to do, you can hear it from the horse's mouth. This song is about my past relationships, and how in this world of 2008 girls are thrown into a lion's den of who's on this team and who's on that team? I was dating this boy who was very metrosexual, I always end up with these guys who are very sensitive and good looking and clean-cut and smell good. But this one in particular, I thought, "In another life, you are a gay man." I'll just leave it at that.'

What about the stereotyping aspect of it all? 'No, I think that there isn't any one type of gay person,' said Katy, still keeping her cool. 'I've met a ton of different gay people. I wasn't stereotyping anyone in particular, I was talking about my ex-boyfriend. All these songs are very personal, they're straight out of a "dear diary" situation . . . [but] my Anne Frank is now being exposed to the world. I'm totally fine with it, I get a lot of messages from girls saying, "I went through the same thing." '

The New Gay cut to the chase: 'Do you have a gay fan base?'

'I'm starting to,' Katy replied. 'My closest friends happen to be gay . . . I came from a very strict household, where any of that taboo stuff was wrong. I don't say I hate where I came from, I love my parents and was happy to . . . have that opportunity to grow, but I came from a strict, suppressed household where that was wrong. Now I've been in LA for seven years and realizing there's nothing wrong, there's nothing wrong with anybody. If you love someone and you're a good person that's what counts.' At this stage, of course, her background wasn't common knowledge, and her parents, while watching from the sidelines, hadn't made any public comment. Whatever their lifestyles were now, they knew about the wider world in which their daughter was making her name.

As time went by, however, Katy began to sound irritated. 'It's obvious that not everybody's gonna hold hands and sing along like they would to "We Are The World",' she snapped to the *Daily Telegraph*. 'But some people look too deeply, like there's a conspiracy or an agenda with songs. Come on, guys, I'm not out there to save the world, I'm just a pop singer.' But pop can be political, and the more famous you are, the more that applies. Katy was learning fast, even if it was through a baptism of fire.

There was also, of course, the accompanying video. Directed by Walter May, it had Katy prancing around in front of a bright, cartoon-like background of clouds with smiley faces drawn on them. The characters in the video are played by Fashion Royalty dolls, and this, at the very least, proves that Katy wasn't trying to take herself too seriously. 'My friend Walter and I were chatting about wanting to do a little video for it a few weeks ago and I said let's use BARBIES! (they're not official Barbies, thank the law!)' Katy wrote on her MySpace page. 'Walter and team spray-painted, wall-papered and even LEATHERED the miniature set . . . I hope you guys pick up on the funny little details . . . like totally awesome rocker dude. Hee hee. We had fun making this.'

All in all, the impression of the video was very much of schoolgirl innocence set against slightly raunchy lyrics: Katy was singing naughty, but coming across clean – a trick she was to perfect on many future occasions. Even the video seemed to cause offence, however, with The New Gay objecting to the fact that the Ken Barbie had no crotch. Was this an implied insult, too? 'I know gay men that are more of a man than some of the men I slept with,' said Katy, who was beginning to sound a little fed up with the line of questioning. 'If it came across like that I didn't mean it. It's kind of like Alanis Morissette's "You Oughta Know", which influenced me so much. I wrote about something very specific and personal to my life. People relate to songs, but this is about my one specific situation.' Poor Katy. It was good preparation for what was to come, though, because none of this would compare with the criticism she would go on to receive when her next single came out.

For a song that wasn't expected to outperform, 'Ur So Gay' didn't do too badly in the charts, getting to No 2 in both the US Hot Singles Sales and the US Hot Dance Singles Sales Billboard charts. And if the A-side and video proved controversial, at least the B-side wasn't. It was a cover of 'Your Love', which was picked because of its danceability. 'There were a couple of choices in the pile for covers,' Katy told Prefix. 'I actually wanted to do a Queen cover, but there wasn't anything they would play in the club. So I'm back to square one, and I go out dancing with my girls. "Use Your Love", the original version by The Outfield, comes on, and immediately every girl hits the dance floor. Everybody's out there dancing and trying to hit these notes. It was the best time, and I wanted to capture that on the track "Ur So Gay".' It was a good choice and one that didn't backfire.

And despite all the controversy, after all these years

Katy was finally getting the chance to see other people listen to her music. Every star remembers the first time they hear themselves on the radio, and the thrill it produces, and Katy was no different. It was a big moment.

'I was on my way, running an errand in Hollywood, and I turn on my radio and I heard them play the Catch of the Day on [LA-based station] KROQ," she told the *Santa Barbara Independent*. 'And it was a song from my EP [called] "Ur So Gay". I literally almost ran into the center divider. I was like, "Not only am I hearing my song for the first time, but I'm hearing my song on KROQ," which is so cool. And I just heard that KJEE added the song, too, and I'm like, "Yeah, hometown hero, let's go!"'

It was nothing compared with the publicity, success and notoriety Katy would shortly receive, but it was a start and, more importantly, it got her noticed by someone very influential indeed. Madonna had been showing her peers how to generate publicity from around the time that Katy was born, and she knew exactly how much weight her words would have when it came to promoting a young singer. So there was nothing accidental about it when Madonna appeared on the KRQ 93.7 Johnjay and Rich morning show and the Ryan Seacrest morning show, and commented that 'Ur So Gay' was her 'favourite song right now'.

In that moment, Katy was on the map. She was well aware that this was the kind of publicity (and kudos) that money couldn't buy: 'I'm still floored by that,' she said afterwards. 'It's like, you're Madonna – you don't have time to be listening to my songs!'

But it seemed she did. It wasn't the first time Madonna had helped a fellow female artiste – several years earlier she'd walked around wearing T-shirts bearing the legend 'Kylie Minogue' – and it has to be said that she did herself no harm by allying herself with someone who was young and cool, and who was clearly the next big thing with a great career ahead of them. To have Madonna's endorsement was not to be sniffed at, though, and consequently Katy found herself in a whole new league.

Katy had also attracted the attention of someone else who would give her career a huge boost from then on in. Perez Hilton – real name Mario Armando Lavandeira Jr; his assumed name is a play on Paris Hilton – was born on 23 March 1978 in Miami and had become one of the world's best-known celebrity bloggers via Perezhilton. com. Perez – who is gay – had become so powerful he seemed able to make or break celebrities depending on what he wrote about them. Absolutely nothing escaped his attention and his reaction could have a major influence on a rising star's career. He noticed Katy, liked what he saw and told the world about her in his own inimitable way. 'If Avril Lavigne were actually talented, pretty and had an appealing personality, she'd be Katy Perry. She's got the whole package!' he announced.

Katy was well aware of what Perez had done for her. 'He's definitely just one of those guys that has that ability to throw something up on the internet and it's like boom, you know?" she told *Beatweek Magazine*. 'The reaction is instant in very large numbers. So he's cool.' And the reaction was another factor that helped make Katy a star.

That was it: Katy had the Perez Hilton endorsement, and it was something she would keep over the years to come. First Perez became a fan and then a friend, and he would pop up constantly in Katy's life (and Katy in his), interviewing her on the red carpet, making videos with her, posting them on his blog and praising her at every opportunity. 'Katy is clearly in her own lane right now,' he told *US Weekly* some years later as her career began to soar. 'So she's being very smart and strategic in how she's positioning herself. And people relate to that, people resonate with authenticity, and that's what's great about Travis [Garland]. He's a real authentic artist, like Gaga and like Katy Perry.'

Perez, who has earned a reputation for being enormously gifted at spotting talent, was certain that Katy was on her way, and he was proved absolutely right. He could see that a woman who was capable of attracting such a huge amount of attention was going to go far. Katy had proved that she could handle potentially difficult situations with aplomb: she had never at any stage lost her temper, had responded politely to criticism and given every impression of being a pro. This is where all those years of paying her dues had come in: now that Katy was finally making a name for herself, she knew how to handle herself in public – far more, in fact, than she would have done had she made it all those years earlier.

And here it was: the big time. People were talking about her and many of them were buying her song. This is what she'd been working towards and now she'd finally got it, though it was going to take a little while to get used to. After so many years of false starts and always being the bridesmaid, never the bride, Katy could scarcely believe it had finally happened.

People were listening to her and buying her music and she was taking the whole thing in her stride. Jason Flom had turned out to be spot on: his new find had star quality in spades, and now that she had the limelight it was coming to the fore. Meanwhile details of Katy's background were beginning to make their way into the public domain, which only helped create more curiosity about this pretty girl from a Christian background, who had released an album of gospel songs before going mainstream and getting seriously controversial.

Katy had worked hard for her success, but that wasn't the only element of her life, even then. Although Katy was never as wild as some commentators liked to assert, she was a very pretty girl and had no problem at all attracting boyfriends. The relationship with Matt Thiessen was long over, but plenty of men were interested in dating Katy and she was just as interested in them.

And so it was that she started on her second relationship, one that was to prove tempestuous, with numerous breaks, reconciliations and partings. Ultimately it wouldn't endure, but it was her only really serious relationship before she met Russell Brand, and it provided her with a life and an interest outside work. His name was Travie McCoy, a fellow musician, and for a couple of years he was Katy Perry's great love.

A Hip-Hop Hero

The year was 2007. Katy Perry was nearing the big time, even if she didn't know it yet, but she also wanted a little fun in her life. If the difference between her first incarnation as Katy Hudson and the present needed highlighting, it's best illustrated through the difference between her first boyfriend and the one she had just started dating, Gym Class Heroes' front man, Travie McCoy. Travie, or Travis as he was known back then, while not exactly a bad boy, grew up in the hip-hop tradition, and had a background that was very different to Katy's Christian upbringing.

Travis Lazarus McCoy was born on 6 August 1981 in Geneva, New York, to a Haitian father and a mother of Irish and Native American ancestry. Passionately interested in both hip hop and art, he got the chance to concentrate on the latter after a skateboarding accident left him in a wheelchair for four months (it's a striking coincidence that Greg Wells, Katy's collaborator on 'Ur So Gay' also spent time in a wheelchair as a child, and in both cases it gave them time to hone their musical skills, paving the way for the profession they would eventually follow). Travis's childhood was not an easy one – in adulthood he's spoken about a person he was close to dying of AIDS when he was still a child – but he became an aficionado of the streets and the art and music it produced.

Throughout his childhood, Travis would visit Manhattan to take part in 'battle raps' – a way of fighting with words rather than weapons. The contestants would rap at one another, boasting about themselves while putting their opponent down. One of the masters of the genre, Big Daddy Kane, wrote a book called *How to Rap*. 'Your mentality is battle format,' he said of battle rapping. 'Your focus was to have a hot rhyme in case you gotta battle someone – not really making a rhyme for a song.' In other words, it was high energy, macho and aggressive, and ideal as a way of learning a trade as a singer/songwriter. It was also very different from Katy's musical background and that of the people who surrounded her.

Travis took up the drums when he was still at school and formed a group called True Life Playas with his father and brother, making recordings of the music they played. The older Travis was a little embarrassed about this: 'It was so bad!' he told Crossfire. 'The tapes exist somewhere but hopefully they'll never be found. In high school I took songwriting and poetry way more seriously; it was a good outlet for me. I used to get grounded a lot for goofing off so that gave me a lot of time to be artistic.'

Like Katy, Travis got involved with music at school. In gym class at Geneva High School he met Matt McGinley, which is where the name Gym Class Heroes originated. 'When I was in the tenth grade, I got transferred to Matt's gym class, and we found out that we were both drummers – at the time, I was the drummer in another punk band,' he told *Seventeen*. 'We just united in gym class and would talk about our favorite drummers and music in general. Then, we ended up playing a mutual friend's birthday party. We didn't have a singer, so I stepped up to the mic, and we've been playing together ever since!'

Music wasn't always Travis's first choice of career, however: after graduating, he studied the arts at the Munson Williams Proctor Arts Institute, majoring in fine arts and illustration. He realized it wasn't what he wanted, though, and dropped out at the age of twenty. His interest in the arts remains strong, however, as witnessed by the album cover he designed: 'I went to an arts school so I majored in fine arts and illustration. I actually came up with the concept of [Gym Class Heroes' third album] *As Cruel as School Children* artwork.'

Extremely creative, Travis was beginning to realize that his first love was music. He had a little way to go before his career took off, but his apprenticeship would be nothing like as long as Katy's. When he was fifteen, Travis started work in a tattoo parlour, and he returned to this job now, as well as teaching by day in the Boys & Girls Club (a philanthropic institution to help youngsters) and slogging in a gas station at night. When that became too much, he quit all three jobs and supported himself by working as an artist. 'My friend and I put together an art show, had friends over and sold a ton of paintings,' he told *Seventeen*. 'It just felt so good to focus on those paintings and sell them and actually have it work. At that point I was like, all right, if I set my mind to it, as cliché as it sounds, I can do whatever I want.'

Travis's musical career took off pretty quickly. The band, which had been chugging away quietly in the background, was going strong and comprised Travis; Matt, the group's drummer; guitarist Disashi Lumumba-Kasongo and bassist Eric Roberts. It didn't take them long to get a record deal, with Fueled by Ramen and Decaydance Records. Unlike Katy, their label actually released a record, *The Papercut Chronicles*, which was a huge success. (Paper cuts, incidentally, are another thing that's very much associated with school, showing that the boys' background was never far from their minds.) They put in a lot of work to promote the album, appearing at festivals such as Bamboozle and the Warped Tour.

In 2006, when Katy was still in the middle of her wilderness years, Gym Class Heroes released the album *As Cruel as School Children*, complete with Travis's artwork. Two versions of the album appeared, the first in July and the second in November, with the second featuring the song 'Cupid's Chokehold', which guest-starred Patrick Stump of Fall Out Boy. A version of the song had appeared on *The Papercut Chronicles* and more versions would follow. In the video for the first version, directed by Andrew Paul Bowser, Travis finds a large doll that comes to life and becomes his girlfriend, before malfunctioning. Travis tries to kill her (neither video is suitable for younger fans!) and thinks he has succeeded after pushing her off a bridge, but then she resurfaces with someone else.

The second video, directed by Alan Ferguson for the second album, has a sweet little Cupid who shoots Travis, making him fall in love with a girl who is ultimately unfaithful to him. After much toing and froing, he ends up with a girl he meets at a bar, who was, of course, played by Katy. 'Cupid's Chokehole' was a massive success and was followed by 'Clothes Off!!!' and 'Cookie Jar', two exuberant numbers aimed at the teen market from which Travis had sprung.

In spite of the humour in the videos there was a dark side to Travis's life at the time, which was only revealed much later, even though it related to his early years. In 2008, on his blog, Travis admitted that he had been addicted to drugs since the age of fifteen, something that Katy was never linked to and which was never referred to at the time. 'Recovering from a relatively new procedure that cleans your opiate receptors and basically gives you a new beginning,' he blogged. 'I feel like a layer of shit has been peeled off of my brain. I'm sure alot of you who really pay attention to our music know that I've been addicted to pharmaceuticals since I was fifteen years old. This is my second stint in a detox program, the first was right before we signed to FBR and it really didn't help much. Meeting after meeting, I still had a thirst, a death wish. F--- it, it is what it is. You're probably asking yourself, "[Why] is he spilling his guts on the inter-web?" Well, the truth of the matter is, I felt an enormous amount of guilt for glorifying drug use in our music, I never talked about getting f---ed up in song to sound cool or to gain points. It was my life, day in day out, it's how I coped with everything.'

Matters had come to a head in 2007 when his cousin Isaiah died and he fell 'face first' into drugs. This was the year in which he met Katy and made those happy videos for 'Cupid's Chokehold', when in reality something much more serious was going on. He blogged about that, too. 'Then people started dropping like flies all around me – friends, Heath, Pimp C, etc., etc.,' he said. 'Still, I was selfish and thought I was invincible, as we all do. I realized something: I gave myself an expiration date, a self-fulfilled destiny I was certain to make true. For some retarded reason I never thought I'd make it past twenty-seven. Well, it's nearing, and I'm still here, and I have no plans to leave anytime soon.' Travis was brave to go so public with it, but it was hardly the lifestyle Katy was used to, although with hindsight it must have helped her understand her future husband, Russell Brand, who, famously, was a heroin addict for years.

This, then, was the man who was to become Katy's first great love. They were together for three years on and off, and it seemed at one point as if they were going to get married – although that was before she met the man who would become her first husband.

As befits a young couple who were working almost constantly, it was work that brought them together. 'We were working with the same producer in New York City,' Katy told one interviewer. 'At the end of my trip – it was just when I first started going to New York and not really knowing anybody – I was like: "Please God, somebody take me out." So I made him take me out. All of his friends were there, and we ended up dancing and making out on the dancefloor.'

Gym Class Heroes had been recording in the same studio as Katy and, given that Travis was a little slow in making a move, Katy was at first unsure if the attraction was mutual. It was – so much so that Travis became besotted and was hit really badly when the pair broke up. In the early days, he was as keen as could be to get involved with Katy on every level: 'When we were talking about who'd play my love interest in the ['Cupid's Chokehold'] video I was like: "I know, why don't we call Katy?"' Travis told one interviewer. 'The rest is history.'

Travis was certainly all man. With his tattoos and hip-hop background, he couldn't have been more different to the boys Katy had hung out with in the past – ironically so, given the title and content of 'Ur So Gay', and the many interviews she had given complaining that the men she dated were effeminate and 'emo'. One thing's for certain, that song wasn't inspired by Travis. Katy was still young, but she was starting to come to terms with her growing sexuality, and something in her responded to Travis in a way she hadn't with anyone before. The two went on to have a properly adult relationship, and the pastor's daughter seemed thrilled to have found such a sexy, macho man.

However, in her choice of Travis as her boyfriend, Katy seemed to be behaving in a manner that was in keeping with her past. He might have been a bad boy rapper, but he was also very protective, and Katy liked that. Deep down, she was a good girl who appreciated being looked after her by her man. 'When I'm with him, he gives off a "don't mess with my girl vibe". And that's really sexy,' she told the *News of the World* in an interview after 'I Kissed A Girl' had made her famous and the media were desperate to find out if she had ever kissed a girl for real. Instead, all they discovered was a macho hip-hop artist. 'He always smells real good. It's not like he is a slob. But he is totally different from guys I've dated in the past. He's not a sensitive, metrosexual guy – he's cheekier than that. Travis is really funny. We have the same sense of humour.' He was also, of course, a drug addict, although Katy seemed to manage to keep herself apart from that side of her new beau.

Katy certainly had a mesmerizing effect on her men. She had grown up within a happy marriage in utmost security: the family might have been poor at times, but she had felt loved and it had given her a proper sense of self-worth. This, combined with her appearance, made her a colossally attractive proposition to the men she met, and Travis was no exception. He was absolutely besotted, and as Katy's profile began to grow and the two emerged as a well-known couple, he often sounded as if he could scarcely believe his luck.

'This is the first time I've been super head-over-heels

about someone since the third grade and almost in the sense where there's this urge in me to pull a Tom Cruise and jump on Oprah's couch,' he told MTV, in reference to the notorious episode in which, proclaiming his love for Katie Holmes, Tom Cruise very nearly ruined his reputation and career by cavorting about on Oprah's sofa in the middle of an interview. 'It's something that I can't escape [from interviewers]. The questions always come up, and I'm never one to be a dick and be like, "I don't want to talk about that." But it's inevitable. People want to know everything and anything they can about you when you're in the spotlight. And even with my music, I don't hide too much. So in that, and in interviews, I try to stay honest.' An admirable stance, perhaps, but it would backfire when the couple publicly split.

While they were together, however, Travis was a very supportive boyfriend, and he was delighted when his girlfriend started to achieve mega-success. 'As soon as Katy played "I Kissed A Girl" to me, I said: "Baby, this is a smash,"' Travis told the *Daily Star*. 'I totally knew from the word go, but she wasn't so sure. She was like: "Do you really think so?" I proved it to her. When Gym Class Heroes went on tour earlier this year we put together a playlist of songs to play before we went on stage. I put 'I Kissed A Girl' on there without Katy knowing, and as soon as it blasted out the kids went absolutely mad. They didn't even know who Katy Perry was then. Katy turned up to one gig while we were playing it and was like: "What are you doing?" She was happy with the reaction though.

Fortunately the rest of Gym Class Heroes love her. She's no Yoko. My bandmates have admitted she's the first girlfriend I've gone out with that they can stand.'

And so matters chugged along, happily enough at first. Even a chance meeting with Russell Brand in 2008 didn't seem to bode ill for the relationship. Travis and Katy worked in the same business, after all, with all the pressures that entailed, the endless touring and search for chart success, the media interviews and the urgent need to stay on top of your game. As we'll see, Katy coped admirably with her first taste of success, but for now a whole new world was opening up for her and she liked what she saw. Travis was also a good sounding board, because he'd already experienced a degree of fame and knew all the pitfalls, so when Katy needed advice, comfort or just a chat, he understood the world she was starting to make her own.

But still – and it is a big but – they were apart. Both artists had to tour in order to promote their records and both had a massively pressurized schedule that didn't leave them with a great deal of free time. Nor were they even based in the same place: while Travis was in New York, Katy was thousands of miles away in LA. In hindsight it might have been sensible for Travis to address that issue before it was too late and they began leading entirely separate lives, but at the time all he could see was that he had a beautiful girlfriend who was becoming a successful singer. It was Katy who was becoming more detached.

Looking back, it's easy to see the warning signs. Katy had all the security of a relationship without needing to make a great deal of effort, since it was physically impossible for her to be with Travis for much of the time. 'I love long-distance relationships,' she told the *News of the World* in another interview, which should have set alarm bells ringing for Travis. 'Absence keeps things exciting. I love my space, and appreciate the moments when we're together. We turn off our phones, cuddle in bed and order in food.'

It was a sweet little picture, but it didn't equate to a full-on relationship with a normal day-to-day routine. Even so, Travis remained blithely unaware of what was to come. He certainly seemed to be thinking in terms of marriage now – very publicly so – presenting Katy with a promise ring. A promise ring is a pre-engagement ring, and it's a tradition that has largely disappeared in Europe, but which continues to flourish in the United States. It seemed as though it was only a matter of time before they would be officially wed.

We know exactly how it came about because Travis, in his besotted state, told everyone. After all, when you're young and in love, you want to share it with the world, and he did, in June 2008. 'I went in [to the jewelry store] and said I wanted a ring,' he told *People*. 'The lady behind the counter said, "Here's one for $300." I was like, "I want a nice ring!" Then I pointed to the big one. I was so scared to give it to her [but] she was so excited! And I'd set up flowers everywhere.' Katy wore it on the third finger of her left hand and Travis wore his own version, too.

Travis could hardly contain himself: Katy was 'super hot', he gushed, and rumours of an engagement were rife – according to some reports Travis had gone down on bended knee in Paris. Official denials were issued, but the rumours spread at such a pace that Katy was forced to deny it in her blog: 'From the horses [sic] mouth, NOT engaged! But thanks for the free press *New York Daily News*! You should fact check with the source before you spread worldwide news like that.' Meanwhile, someone had read Travis's comments about the ring wrongly and was putting it about that Katy's ring had only cost $300, to which Travis replied that he was 'insulted'.

There were signs, however, that Travis, rather than Katy, was having a difficult time with what Lady Gaga would call 'the fame'. In July 2008, at a concert in St Louis, a member of the audience shouted racial abuse at him. Instead of ignoring it, which would have been the sensible course of action, not least because security men ended up dragging the culprit out, Travis demanded, 'What did you just call me?' According to some reports, he brought the man up on stage and hit him with the microphone. His spokesman later said that it had been in self-defence as the man hit him first in the knee area. His annoyance was understandable, but unwise: public figures have to put up with being called an awful lot of things, and the only way to deal with it is to ignore it. Instead, Travis ended up getting arrested.

It was around this time that he started talking about his drug use. It's far more difficult than most people realize to be constantly in the public eye, perhaps even more so when you have a high-profile partner, and Katy was beginning to show signs of becoming even more successful than Travis.

The pair continued to see one another whenever they could, but behind the scenes tensions were mounting. There were arguments, bickering and unhappiness and nowhere near enough time to talk about it face to face. Towards the end of 2008, the couple had a holiday in Mexico together, but what was really going on behind the scenes only came to light when Travis posted an entry on his blog. It was lyrics from the song 'Looking At The Front Door' by the hip-hop group Main Source and it was very telling: 'We fight every night, now that's not kosher/I reminisce with bliss of when we was closer.' There was a lot more where that came from, and the next post read, 'My Laptop is my new bitch. LOYAL. LISTENS. and NEVER LETS ME DOWN.'

There was clearly trouble in paradise, and it therefore came as no surprise when the split was announced. Katy was seen in tears in Mexico, and there seemed to be anger and bitterness on both sides. Suddenly the downside of being such a public couple became apparent: apart from some blogging, neither party seemed to want to talk about it, and yet interest in them remained as strong as ever. Both gave the odd reluctant answer when forced to, but neither was particularly forthcoming. Publicity is a double-edged sword, as they were finding out the hard way.

Apart from this, though, Katy had had a magnificent year. She might have lost a boyfriend, but she'd gained the career she'd been chasing for so long and the world was finally at her feet. Katy had never had the slightest difficulty in attracting men, and now that she was back on the market she was getting a lot of admiration. Was she sad? Yes. But it wasn't long before she started to rally. It had been a serious relationship, but she coped with its demise remarkably well. 'When you break up with someone, you move on,' she told *People*. 'You don't really want to move on . . . but you have to because they don't give you any choice. But I'm over it!'

There was a slight note of wistfulness on her blog. 'So, my post tonight started very melancholy,' she wrote. 'The usual. Mostly just a pity party I suppose. We all throw them . . . no one ever comes, though, especially [to] mine.'

There were plenty of people who were happy to come to any other party Katy might want to throw, however. There were rumours linking her to Benji Madden, which were promptly and hotly denied: 'It's two pseudo famous people sitting next to each other . . .' she wrote on her blog. 'Doesn't mean we were bumping uglies! You know I don't just do that with anyone! I was there celebrating a really fun show and a boozy Valentine's Day with all my good friends. We were like a group of 25! Benji is a nice young fellow, but my heart really belongs to kitty purry/ markus molinari.' (Kitty Purry was her cat.) There was a public vow of chastity, with Kitty Purry the only recipient of any Katy kiss. If anything, she was off the male sex: 'Fuck boys!' she cried to a cheering audience on Valentine's Day. 'We don't need boys – we got girls.'

In the meantime, it was becoming apparent that Travis was really suffering from the split, so much so that he managed to talk Katy round and, in April 2009, the two briefly resumed their relationship. Travis was delighted. 'The break-up sucked,' he told the *Sun*. 'We're back together now. I keep thinking about if I had to go through it again and how shitty it would be. We were moving way too fast. I was being juvenile about the whole thing. Now it's easy breezy. I'm happy and in love. I'm just enjoying the way things are right now. I'm in no rush to get the ball and chain strapped to my legs.'

By which he meant get married, but to be honest, Travis should have been so lucky. The relationship staggered on for a couple more months before finishing for good, and Katy went on to hook up straight away with another bad boy, leaving Travis to nurse his broken heart.

It really was broken, too. One of his first actions after the split was to get everyone to call him Travie, not Travis, as a symbol of a fresh start. It didn't stop him brooding, though, and being in the public eye didn't help. A full year after the break-up he gave an interview to *Today*, in which he still sounded somewhat raw: 'Usually I just tell my publicist to tell whoever's interviewing me to not bring it up,' he confessed. '[But] it usually does anyway. I'm a nice dude, I'm pretty easygoing about it if it does get brought up, but honestly, it's been a year and some change, you know. Like, I'm over it. There's no bad blood. I wish her nothing but the best in her future endeavors. I'm not the type to hold grudges. Why would I? Our time together was awesome and it's time to move on. And we both have gone our separate ways so it is what it is. We haven't really talked much since the demise of our relationship. I've since relocated and started over.'

Travie had relocated to Miami, but that wasn't the end of it, because in May 2010, it emerged that Travie had been working on a mix tape called *Forgetting Katy Perry*. By now Katy was well and truly ensconced with Russell Brand, who had made a film called *Forgetting Sarah Marshall*, about getting over a break-up, and Travie made no bones about what the music was about. 'Me, personally as an artist, I just write about my life,' he told *Rap-Up*. 'Unfortunately, that involves going through break-ups. Sometimes it makes for really, really good music and sometimes it makes for sad and depressing shit. To an extent, I'm comfortable with discussing it, but when it becomes the main focus, I'm like, "Aight, let's just keep going." This shit is out for public consumption anyway. In the beginning it was our relationship, but after a while it turned into everyone else's relationship. On those gossip blogs, everyone has their views on our relationship. I'm over it.'

That wasn't quite the impression he was giving, however. In another interview, some very hurt feelings emerge, not least about the speed with which Katy moved on. Even the fact that Travie was giving interviews said a lot: it seemed that he wasn't just getting the pain out through his music, but by talking abut Katy non-stop, too. Katy had moved on in her personal life and comprehensively over-taken him career-wise, so it's hardly surprising that he felt a little upset.

'It was hinting more to the career aspect but not to throw stones, but I think it was inspired by that whole situation,' he told *Complex* magazine. 'At the end of the day, I think anyone who has been through some shit can relate to ["Don't Pretend"]. It could have been about my girl-friends before, but I'ma [sic] keep it real with you, it was definitely about Katy Perry. I definitely felt a certain way about the whole situation. Having a year and a half to reflect on it, you start questioning everything . . . The time-lines . . . she got engaged so quickly after. I was like, 'Really?' I had to sit back and reassess what was really going on. After you have some time to start thinking about it, you start putting things together. It's been a year and a half. I'm over it. I'm sure she knows. The mixtape is not airing out any dirty laundry. If anything, it's me poking fun at myself. If you've seen *Forgetting Sarah Marshall*, that's my life. I'm that dude.'

He was true to his word: although the mix tape was plainly about Katy, there was no viciousness and no secrets were spilled.

Katy was beyond all that now, though. Not only had she

tamed the once wild-living Russell Brand, who had cut quite a swathe through the female population in the years before he met her, she had become one of the most famous pop stars in the world. And it was all down to one little song . . .

'I Kissed A Girl'

It was early 2008 and a buzz was building around Katy. 'Ur So Gay' might not have set the world on fire, but it had introduced her to the record-buying public for the first time, and the music industry was beginning to realize that a hot new property might be about to emerge. The events surrounding her initial assault on the charts were planned with military precision, whilst the look Katy had been cultivating for so long – part Japanese gamine character, part 1950s high-school girl – was proving attractive to both sexes: men fancied her and women wanted to be her friend. Now that the single and EP had been released and performed perfectly respectably, everyone was ready to make the big leap.

That leap, of course, was 'I Kissed A Girl', which was put out as a single from Katy's first album, *One of the Boys*. The risk the record company was taking was phenomenal. If 'Ur So Gay' had had people up in arms, how would a song about sapphic experiences play with middle America? If they got this one wrong, they'd blown it.

It was a risk the record company was prepared to take. 'When she was cutting "I Kissed A Girl", she comes into my office and plays me the song on her guitar,' Chris Anokute told HitQuarters. 'I thought, oh my god, if the music is incredible then this is a career record. I couldn't wait to start playing it to people in the office, but for some reason people weren't getting it. One influential senior exec told me it sounded like an international club track. Other people said, "This is never going to get played on the radio. How do we sell this? How's this going to be played in the Bible belt?"

'I was 24 – I know what young people out there listen to. I've partied and hung out socially with Katy and her friends, and I knew how she responded to music, so I kept on fighting. I convinced one of the radio guys to believe in the record. Dennis Reese [Senior Vice President at the label] saw the vision. So I had to use him to try to convince everyone to give this record a shot. So we have one shot – if this doesn't go Katy is probably going to get dropped. We have to make a statement. Dennis Reese helps me to push the record as a single. The first station to play Katy's single was The River in Nashville. They took a chance and after playing it for three days, they were innundated with enthusiastic calls. A star was born.'

The song did what it said on the label: it talked about kissing a girl in pretty innocuous terms. 'Us girls we are so magical/Soft skin, red lips, so kissable.'

'I Kissed A Girl' was one of the numbers Katy had worked on with Dr Luke, together with Max Martin and Cathy Dennis, and it mirrored the experiences of a lot of teens who had kissed a girlfriend before moving on to boys. Scarlett Johansson, who has particularly luscious lips, was said to have been one inspiration behind it, to which she replied, 'That's flattering, but my lips are kind of taken.' She had just married the actor Ryan Reynolds when she learned about being Katy's muse. 'I had no idea. I should get a cut,' she joked.

Then Katy added to the fun by saying that it had been based on personal experience. 'The song was inspired by a friendship I had with a girl when I was fifteen, and I did kiss her,' she told *Q* magazine. 'I was totally obsessed with her. She was beautiful – porcelain skin, perfect lips – and I still talk to her, but I've never told her the song is about her.'

Of course, every new release has to be accompanied by a video, and this one was no different. Directed by Kinga Burza, Katy's video took place somewhere that looked like the Moulin Rouge, with lots of flamboyantly dressed women dancing around, although they're not actually kissing one another, before Katy wakes up next to a bloke called Derek (the DJ Skeet Skeet). The video also featured the DJ Mia Moretti, who was a friend of Katy's, and the then totally unknown Ke$ha.

The New Gay, which had been so down on 'Ur So Gay', was very keen to know what the message behind the song was. 'Everyone takes the song and relates it to their situation, they can see it however they want to see it,' Katy said enigmatically. 'Love it, hate it, for me it was about us girls. When we're young, we're very touchy-feely. We have slumber party sing-a-longs, we make up dance routines in our pajamas. We're a lot more intimate in a friendship than guys can be. It's not perverse but just sweet, that's what the song is about . . .'

The song caused a sensation, and for the first time in her life Katy was getting a huge amount of attention – and reviews – from the music press. 'You may have heard her new single, "I Kissed A Girl",' wrote Garon Cockrell on Blogcritics. 'It appears to be on everyone's mind and with good reason. It's an instantly catchy number. That track is backed up by eleven other equally great tracks on her just released album, *One of the Boys*. The 23-year-old Santa Barbara, CA native has expertly crafted an album full of standout songs. From the upbeat opening title track to the rocking closing track, "Fingerprints", Katy Perry has given us what is probably the most unexpected pop success of the year.' She'd certainly waited for long enough.

'It was only a matter of time before the wit and style of British female singer-songwriters Lily Allen and Kate Nash landed on American shores,' wrote Bill Lamb on About.com. 'A distinctly US born version has arrived in the person of Katy Perry. Her single "I Kissed A Girl" is burning up charts, both sales and airplay, and [now the public should] look for more sassy women to vie for the pop spotlight she has so expertly snatched.'

However, not everyone was so enthusiastic. Stephen Thomas Erlewine, on Allmusic, hated it. 'All the pros give *One of the Boys* a cross-platform appeal, but there's little question that its revolting personality is all down to Katy Perry, who distills every reprehensible thing about the age of The Hills into one pop album,' he snapped. 'She disses her boyfriend with gay-baiting; she makes out with a girl and she doesn't even like girls; she brags to a suitor that he can't afford her, parties till she's face-down in the porcelain, drops brands as if they were weapons, curses casually, and trades under-the-table favors. In short, she's styled herself as a Montag monster. Perry is not untalented – she writes like an ungarbled Alanis and has an eye for details, as when she tells her emo metrosexual boyfriend to hang himself with his H&M scarf on "Ur So Gay" – but that only accentuates how her vile wild-child persona is an artifice designed to get her the stardom she craves.' It was a harsh judgement, and one that was in the minority, but it showed that not everyone was swept away by this bright new star.

Sal Cinquemani, in online magazine Slant, was equally down on the album. 'This generation's concept of being edgy and provocative is tame and retrograde,' stormed Sal, drawing an unfavourable comparison with the young Madonna. 'Perry confuses political incorrectness with being subversive on tracks like "Hot N Cold", in which she, in the process of skewering guys who change their minds "like girls change clothes", just winds up sounding mildly sexist. Lead single "I Kissed A Girl" features a throbbing beat and an infectious, bi-curious hook, but its self-satisfied, in-your-face posturing rings phony in comparison to the expertly constructed ambiguities of "Justify My Love" or practically anything in the first decade of Ani DiFranco's catalogue; it's like a tween version of DiFranco's tortured bisexual confession "Light Of Some Kind". "I Kissed A Girl" isn't problematic because it promotes homosexuality, but because its appropriation of the gay lifestyle exists for the sole purpose of garnering attention – both from Perry's boyfriend and her audience.'

And so it went on. Some critics adored it, others loathed it, but few ignored it. And as details about Katy's Christian background began to emerge, it aroused a good deal of curiosity about the singer herself. Controversy about the subject matter of the song was beginning to grow – although it was clear that Katy had been with Travis for some time – and there was a further moue from the music industry when someone pointed out that the title wasn't original; it was also the title of a song released by Jill Sobule in 1995.

Katy was slightly dismissive of any confusion that might cause. 'The 14 and 15 year old girls don't know who Jill Sobule is, but I'm sure Jill Sobule is gonna make some money this year in iTunes,' Katy told *Beatweek Magazine*. 'I was thinking about should I name it, like, "Cherry Chapstick" or something? And I was just like, no, it is what it is.'

She wasn't being entirely realistic about Jill's take on it. In July 2009, Jill finally broke her long silence. 'When Katy Perry's song came out I started getting tons of inquiries about what I thought,' she told The Rumpus. 'Some folks (and protective friends) were angry, and wondered why she took my title and made it into this kind of "girls gone wild" thing . . . As a musician I have always refrained from criticizing another artist. I was, "Well, good for her." It did bug me a little bit, however, when she said she came up with the idea for the title in a dream. In truth, she wrote it with a team of professional writers and was signed by the very same guy that signed me in 1995. I haven't mentioned that in interviews as I don't want to sound bitter or petty . . . Okay, maybe, if I really think about it, there were a few jealous and pissed-off moments. So here goes, for the first time in an interview . . .' The following Jill said as a joke, 'Fuck you, Katy Perry, you fucking stupid, maybe "not good for the gays", title-thieving, haven't heard much else, so not quite sure if you're talented, fucking little slut.'

Katy could afford to rise above it. 'I Kissed A Girl' debuted on the Billboard Hot 100 at No 76, eventually rising to No 1. Various other records were broken, too, as it made history by reaching the No 1 spot on Billboard's Hot Dance Airplay chart by week three, a first for a solo act with a debut single. Over in the UK, it sold over 635,000 copies, the first Virgin single to do so since the Spice Girls' 'Goodbye' in 1998 – while it also got to No 1 in various other countries all over the world. Shortly afterwards there were cover versions from The Saturdays, Nicki Bliss and Barnicle, and the song even featured in the pilot episode of *Glee*, while spoof versions of it made it into the charts.

It was all Katy could have wished for and more. There were growing rows over whether or not she was promoting homosexuality, and whether she should be flirting with faux lesbianism, but the controversy just helped to fuel publicity, which in turn promoted album sales. Mostly, that is. The record was banned in some countries, such as Singapore, because of the subject matter, but it continued to ratchet up sales elsewhere.

All of this led to growing interest in Katy's past, as

exemplified in this early profile on Plugged In Online. 'The business of predicting a young musician's trajectory is murky stuff,' it began. 'Just ask *Christianity Today* music reviewer Russ Breimeier. In 2001, when he reviewed then 16-year-old Katy Hudson's self-titled contemporary Christian music debut, he concluded, "Katy Hudson. Trust me, you'll be hearing [that name] more and more." Little did Russ know how right he'd be . . . albeit with plot twists he never anticipated. Fast-forward seven years, and Katy is indeed this moment's It Girl. But getting there necessitated an extreme makeover. The songstress traded in her last name – goodbye Katy Hudson, hello Katy Perry – and jettisoned her Christian music aspirations in exchange for big-time fame and fortune. In place of the teenage prayers in her early song "Piercing" she now brags about her same-sex experimentation in "I Kissed A Girl".'

Unsurprisingly, within the evangelical Christian community that had once claimed Katy as its own, there was a palpable sense of shock. Looking at it from several years distance, it's hard to come to the conclusion that the song was promoting homosexuality – it was just a bit of fun – but Katy was new to the scene, and to outsiders it appeared as if a pretty girl had popped out of nowhere and started singing lyrics that were almost bound to offend the circles in which she once moved. There was, in some ways, a sense of betrayal from some quarters and the reactions of her detractors veered between sadness and fury.

'What a sad picture of a lost child who has been swept away by the carnal pleasures of the world,' was one not untypical blog on the Christian website Planet Wisdom. 'We need to be lifting this gal up in prayer. While we're at it, let's toss up a prayer for her parents, too. Not to mention the countless young girls who will buy into this lesbian chic message.'

Not for the first time, Katy was forced on the defensive. If she'd had to take a lot of stick for 'Ur So Gay', that was nothing compared to what she was putting up with now, and it came from all sides. Genuine lesbians were irritated that she was getting publicity for a lifestyle that wasn't actually hers; Christians were unhappy about the whole thing, and even plain old family rights campaigners felt it wasn't the right message to be sending out to the world.

Katy was caught between two opposing schools of thought, and she may well be the only person in the world who's managed to attract ire from both Christians and gay rights groups for exactly the same song. Even those who weren't accusing her of anything weren't exactly praising her to the skies.

'I don't think she's being homophobic,' said Jane Czyzselska, editor of lesbian magazine *Diva*. 'I think she might be a bit dumb . . . a bit unself-aware. The kind of behaviour you get from some privileged people – "oh I didn't realize". Perhaps she doesn't know any gay people who have suffered verbal or physical abuse.'

One person who did stand up for her was the singer k.d. Lang. k.d. is one of the world's most famous lesbians, having outed herself decades before it was considered acceptable or mainstream, and although she too has been irritated by straight women pretending to be gay or bisexual, she took a more reasonable approach to the new kid on the block. Whilst she didn't offer wholehearted support, she did point out that an awful lot of people got jumpy when Katy was about.

'The Britney-Madonna kiss [at the MTV music awards in 2003] annoyed me,' she told the *Guardian*. 'I don't know much about Katy Perry, but I think there needs to be some "inning" now and then. Ultimately though, it's all good to play with sexuality and not be the gayest gay and not be the straightest straight. Ultimately, we're all bisexual, honestly I think that's true. I think [the gay community's] fears and expectations are the things that get all flustered when someone like Katy Perry has a song.'

Still, quite a few people took a considerably less reasonable line. Much emphasis was placed on how this was hurting Katy's parents, a charge that clearly stung. 'Well, I'm not strung out on crack and doing centrefolds,' she snapped. As for the song itself, she remained defiant. 'The fact of the matter is that girls, a lot of the time, smell much better than boys,' she said. 'We smell like vanilla. We smell like watermelon. We smell like strawberries. So, duh! One day I was with my boyfriend and I opened up a magazine and realized, "You know what, honey, I would probably make out with Angelina Jolie if she wanted to." It doesn't matter if you're female or male, if the right woman walks through the door, everybody's jaw is going to be on the floor.'

These comments didn't help her case, though. All this

controversy was fast turning Katy into a household name, but as she became more and more famous, people became increasingly curious about her background, and the more they discovered about her Christian past, the more incredible her u-turn seemed. 'She didn't transition – she stopped dead, reinvented herself, became an artist who has nothing to do with Christian music,' said Joe Levy, editor of *Blender*, which frequently ran articles on Katy. 'It looks like who she is now is who she wants to be, slightly outrageous and very cute.'

In truth, Katy seemed a little schizophrenic about the issue. Of course, she could never have predicted what a huge success the song would become, and while she was, by now, a veteran of the music business, she was also a little too young to understand how much the contrast between her past and her present was likely to shock. She continually prevaricated: one minute she retorted that the last thing she was going to do was go round kissing girls, and the next she was doing just that – a lesbian fan by the name of Jenna Buhmann was the recipient of a smacker during a concert in Washington. Was Katy gay? No. Was she bi? No. But it seemed she couldn't resist stirring things up a little, even though anyone who knew anything about her was fully aware of the fact that at the time of the song's release Travis was still in the background, watching his girlfriend's career soar.

Worse was to come, though; when Katy's parents were asked directly for their views, the message was an uncompromising one: 'I hate the song,' Mary told the *Daily Mail*.

'It clearly promotes homosexuality and its message is shameful and disgusting. Katy knows how I feel. We are a very outspoken family and she knows how disappointed her father and I are. I can't even listen to that song. The first time I heard it I was in total shock. When it comes on the radio I bow my head and pray. Katy is not a homosexual, but I fear she has been led astray by the Hollywood crowd. She is our daughter and we love her and can't cut her out of our lives, but we strongly disagree with how she is conducting herself and she knows how disappointed we are. She changed when she went to LA and is going through a period of rebellion. She's told me, "Oh Mum, I'm not going to turn into Amy Winehouse." But I pray all the time God will help her find salvation.'

In actual fact, Katy and her family never really fell out at any stage and her parents, also unused to dealing with a daughter in the spotlight, were simply not as cautious with the press as they should have been. That didn't stop Mary's quote from making headlines all over the world. Katy was now in the position not only of having to cope with sudden and totally expected fame, but of having to deal with being publicly told off by her parents. No one likes to upset their mother and father, or at least Katy didn't, even if she was now in her twenties. Fame clearly had a downside that she hadn't properly appreciated before.

In some ways it was surprising the Hudsons hadn't spoken out before now. 'Ur So Gay', while having nothing like the same impact as 'I Kissed A Girl', had certainly attracted attention, and its language, if nothing else, was not the kind that they would approve of. The Hudsons' comments came so late because they'd been away preaching in Malaysia when their daughter finally hit the big time. They had therefore missed the beginnings of her sensational rise to fame, and it was only now that the song was making headlines around the world that they realized what a massive story it had become.

In spite of their comments, Katy would not hear a word against them. 'They're great,' she told the *Observer*. Her life might have changed, but she had always had a close and warm relationship with them and nothing would change that. While Katy was no longer actively evangelical, she still held on to her Christian beliefs (and still does). 'I mean, they still pray for me,' she continued. 'They have their thoughts on who I will be and what they want me to be. But I have my own thoughts on that, too. I stopped trying to change them at 21, because I was like: "You're happy. You love what you do, and I respect that. You're living your life and I'm living mine." They've always known I had a big mouth, and a kind of quirky outlook on life.'

It was that same 'quirky outlook' that was helping Katy stand out from the crowd. It was all coming together now: the beautiful pastor's daughter singing a mildly suggestive song; the back story about the years of struggle and getting dropped by record labels over and over again; the fact that Katy was pretty and buzzy and not afraid of speaking out. And, of course, there were the cute clothes, the immaculate make-up and her sense of freshness and fun.

Katy began to discover that, as only the truly famous

A demure Katy Hudson
back when she was forging
her career as a Christian
music singer

Matthew Thiessen, the lead singer of Christian band Relient K, was Katy's first serious boyfriend and a world apart from the wild Russell Brand

Twenty-year-old Katy struggled for years before making it

Christian metal band P.O.D., with whom Katy worked on her rise to fame

Jennifer Knapp: Katy's mentor and manager during her early years

Dr Luke: the prodigious songwriter and producer behind Britney's unforgettable debut 'Baby, One More Time', who co-produced Katy's singles 'California Gurl' and 'Teenage Dream'

Jason Flom, Chairman and CEO of the Atlantic Records Group and legendary music-industry executive: he championed Katy and propelled her into the big time

Glen Ballard: the Grammy award-winning songwriting legend, who was convinced Katy would become a star

It took Katy a while to develop the colourful and eccentric look she's famous for today

Katy used to Super Glue the tips of her fingers to ease the pain of strumming her guitar all day long

Right: On the cusp of stardom . . .

Katy wasn't always the natural performer she is today, although her stage presence was electric from the start

Her on-off relationship with Travis McCoy became increasingly tumultuous, particularly when Katy's career overtook his

Katy appeared on the Gym Class Heroes' video *Cupid's Chokehold*, playing lead singer Travis's love interest

A natural beauty – Katy promoting her Australian concert tour

can, she could make headlines simply through what she was wearing. If a juicy quote was thrown in, then all to the good. At the same time, however, she was beginning to suffer the loss of privacy that all famous people go through, the knowledge that she could no longer walk down a street without being recognized, and that it was important always to be nice and polite. Stars have always had that, of course, but in an age of mobile phones with cameras, Katy found she was constantly on display, constantly being talked about and – given that she blogged – constantly followed online, too. Under the circumstances she coped perfectly well, but these were all considerations she wouldn't have even thought about just a few short months earlier.

With all this going on, it was hardly surprising when Katy confided to one gossip columnist that she could do with some advice from Madonna, a woman who had been through something similar and managed to survive. Madonna had seemed to burst onto the scene overnight, and no one could cause controversy quite like her when she put her mind to it. 'I really wanna have a sitdown dinner with Madonna,' Katy said. 'I'm waiting for that open invitation. I wanna ask her how she's made it through all of this and still continues. It's probably a lot of centring, diet and focus, and self-control, but if she would just give me a little advice – I really wanna pick her brain.'

She certainly needed something to help counter the growing madness that surrounded her. There was Travis, of course, who could understand some of the pressure, but he had never enjoyed the sort of success Katy was experiencing, so wasn't best placed to tell her how to cope. Her musical success was some consolation, though, and she continued to break records by holding on to the No 1 slot.

When Katy was allowed to talk about anything other than the controversial nature of 'I Kissed A Girl', what she said made a great deal of sense. She had been in the business for a long time and had managed to carve out a niche that was pretty unique to her – and it wasn't just as a straight woman singing about kissing girls. Katy's image, for all the girl kissing and glamour, was actually pretty conservative: she was feminine and proud of it. 'I saw a void in the music industry for a movement of female artists that were unapologetic, had something to say, were a bit rock 'n' roll and a bit pop,' she said. 'It wasn't contrived rock, where I just put on a studded belt. That's bull. It was like Joan Jett, Pat Benatar, Cyndi Lauper – all those girls – and then there wasn't any more of those. I mean, there was Shirley Manson, Alanis Morissette and The Cranberries – but that was all in the Nineties.' What the world needed now was a bright, brash and bubbly pop star and that's what Katy was proving to be.

Even before it was released in the UK, Katy's single was making headlines in Britain as much as in the US. The *Observer* sent Sheryl Garratt to find out about this new musical phenomenon that everyone was talking about, and by the time she tracked her down, Katy seemed to have given up defending herself and started talking common sense.

She acknowledged that the fuss the song was causing was totally out of proportion (although it certainly didn't hurt sales) and that she was resigned to how ridiculous the rest of the world was being. She also made another very good point: that girls often start off kissing one another because they're scared of boys. It's the same reason that most male teen idols tend to be slightly feminine: young girls find overt masculinity threatening, and there's nothing new about that.

'I'm talking about the way girls are really touchy-feely and sisterly,' Katy explained. 'Especially when we're growing up. We're holding hands, we're having sleepovers, we're doing choreographed dance moves in our pyjamas, we're painting each other's nails and practising kissing on our arms – or maybe practising kissing on one another. It wasn't something that we were doing for the sake of anybody else because we were scared of boys. I know I was scared of boys! My first kiss was with a boy, and he almost swallowed me alive. I wish I had kissed that girl I had the girl-crush on when I was growing up. I would have been much more prepared for my dating life, I think. What happened to being rock 'n' roll? I play music, I'm not running for President. If only the world would stop walking on eggshells and get a sense of humour. Everyone has their shield up and they're just like: "Offend me! I'm ready to be offended!"'

There was a huge amount of truth in what she said, but Katy was beginning to grow a hard shell. She had to. If you're going to be in the public eye, whether or not you're singing about kissing girls, you're going to attract some flak and the people who are successful quickly learn to deal with it. Katy had caused an uproar with both of her first singles and had put up with an awful lot, including people saying she had let down her parents and her church. The only way to deal with it was to laugh at the detractors and look at her bank account, because whatever anyone said, the record was still at the top of the charts across the world and Katy was fast turning into a global sensation. Everyone wanted a piece of her. She was a breath of fresh air.

Whether Katy liked it or not, however, there were expectations that went with the territory. Any young person with a high public profile will always be judged by the effect they have on their fans. 'I'm not here to be a role model personality,' Katy protested. 'I'm here to be in the business of rock 'n' roll. That means having an attitude, being sexy, being edgy and being unapologetic unless I do something wrong. I look up to people like Joan Jett, Pat Benatar, Freddie Mercury and Cyndi Lauper. I want to have that type of appeal. If folk want a role model they have Miley Cyrus.'

Fighting talk, but it was in vain. Katy was a massively popular twenty-something pop star – who was firmly in the pop, rather than rock, camp – and she was going to be judged on her actions from here on in. It's the price every person in her position has to pay. But despite what some people were saying about her, Katy is essentially a nice, hardworking girl who had to wait many years for pop stardom and was never really going to scare the horses, or anything else come to that.

If they wanted a role model, in reality Katy is far more traditional than she looks. Like so many women, she didn't just want a career, she wanted marriage and motherhood. Her relationship with Travis was still limping along, but at the height of the controversy surrounding her, Katy was about to meet a real bad boy, one whom she appeared to have no trouble taming. Millions of women around the world went into mourning when they heard about it, because this bad boy was also a major sex symbol. His name? Russell Brand.

When Katy Met Russell

In the summer of 2008 Katy Perry was the hottest thing on the planet. Her breakout hit, 'I Kissed A Girl', might have been controversial, but it also established Katy as a massive star. Everything she touched seemed to turn to gold, so it was no surprise when the producers of a film called *Get Him to the Greek* got in touch. Would Katy be interested in a cameo role? Sure she would.

Get Him to the Greek was actually a sequel of sorts – same stars but not all of them had identical roles – to the film *Forgetting Sarah Marshall*. The plot isn't of particular interest here, but suffice to say that one of its stars was the controversial, promiscuous ex-junkie Russell Brand. Having established himself in the UK, Russell had moved to the United States in the hope of making a name for himself, and so far he had met with some success. After *Forgetting Sarah Marshall* did well, Russell was asked to reprise his role as the anarchic pop star Aldous Snow, while Katy accepted a small role in the film.

The impact the two of them had on each other was immediate. Not only was there an incredibly strong attraction, there was a connection, too. More importantly, though, unlike the battalions of women who had fallen at Russell's feet in the past, Katy stood up to him. It seemed that for the first time Russell had met his match. Only someone as confident as Katy could have taken on a man like Russell, not that either of them realized yet what it would lead to. After all, Katy was still officially with Travis and Russell was, well, with everyone else.

Russell certainly seemed to enjoy filming, although Katy wasn't the only person he talked about while filming. 'I had to film three scenes with Pink, Christina Aguilera and Katy Perry,' he told the *Mirror*. 'It was amazing. I've got a soft spot for Pink and I had to kiss her. We have this scene where we are walking down the road snogging and then I have to be sick. Not nice. When you are in a relationship with an actress you don't want them to be having sex scenes. When I was kissing Pink I was thinking, This isn't work. Those kisses were unprofessional. I quite enjoyed that. In the scene with Katy Perry, who is really charming, we are on a balcony of a hotel in Rome berating the paparazzi below, kissing and then I wee out of the window. I didn't kiss Christina but she is a living doll.'

In the end the cameo with Katy was dropped because by the time the film was released a couple of years later, Katy and Russell were a real-life couple, and showing them on screen together would have destroyed the illusion of Russell as Aldous Snow. It wasn't until filming was done, as is often the case in showbusiness circles, that they enjoyed their first kiss, although the spark was definitely there on set. 'My scene called for me to make out with him,' Katy later told *Glamour* magazine. 'And on the way down the stairs after the scene, I was hopping like a bunny.

I hop like a bunny when I'm happy – I get a bit childlike. He gives me the Christmas Eve jitters.' It was obvious that she could sense that something exciting was about to happen, and she was right – though not yet. If Katy had managed to shock the world when she sang about kissing girls, that was nothing compared with the reaction she would provoke when she got together with Russell. From the outside, at least, they made a very odd pair.

Russell Edward Brand was born on 4 June 1975, the only child of Barbara Elizabeth (née Nichols) and Ronald Henry Brand, a photographer. He had a difficult childhood, about as far away from the love and security that surrounded Katy as it's possible to imagine: his parents separated when he was six months old and his mother brought him up alone.

It wasn't all bad, though. From early on, Russell showed signs of being very intelligent and, tellingly, he was a loving little boy. 'Before he was two, Russell was already talking; he was also a very affectionate child,' his mother told *The Sunday Times*. 'One of his favourite books was *Pinocchio*, and one Christmas I bought him a Pinocchio puppet. But he didn't have it more than five minutes when he cut the strings off. I didn't tell him off, but I asked him why he'd done it, and he told me it was because he couldn't cuddle him properly. I mean, my heart just melted. To be honest, although he could be wilful, it was hard for me to be angry with him, and the problem with sending him up to his room was that he didn't see it as a punishment at all. He'd go up and play or sit on his bed and start reading.'

Already a lonely child, matters were made worse when, at the age of eight, Russell's mother contracted uterine cancer. Though it was cured, she went on to develop breast cancer a year later. While she was treated for the disease Russell stayed with relatives, but the disruption and unhappiness took their toll and by the age of fourteen, he was bulimic. Two years later, almost unbelievably, Barbara was diagnosed with cancer for a third time, and this time it was in the lymph nodes. Again she underwent treatment, and Russell was left in the care of her then boyfriend, with whom he didn't get on, so in the end, Russell left home.

'It was an awful time,' he told *The Sunday Times*. 'And I think it was really this third time that affected me the most. I was sixteen, so I was that bit older, and I knew more about what was going on, what it meant. And I guess at the back of my mind I couldn't stop thinking that if someone keeps getting cancer they're going to die. I think in some sense I'd made the decision that she, the person who'd been the constant reference point in my life, just wasn't going to be around any more. And all those thoughts, well, it was just too much.'

It was at this point that he began taking drugs and started down a road that would get him into a lot of trouble. He was pretty liberal in his inclinations, taking cannabis, amphetamines, LSD, ecstasy, cocaine, crack and heroin. Now it was his mother's turn to be out of her mind with worry. 'By now I was just of the attitude that all life's painful and miserable, so why not take them?' Russell said. 'That's why so many people do. Who can blame them?

It's a miracle more people don't. The wonderful thing was that Mum got through all of that. But she then had to deal with me getting into trouble, whether it was coming down to get me from a police station or taking me to a hospital to have tests for things that she should never have had to be involved in. She probably used to look at me and think I was highly talented one day and mentally ill the next.'

Russell's father didn't help matters, either. Twice remarried, he saw Russell only occasionally and, bizarrely, during one trip to the Far East with his son, he took Russell to visit some prostitutes.

There was one saving grace, however: Russell was turning out to be extremely talented theatrically. He attended Grays School Media Arts College, where he made his theatrical debut at fifteen, playing Fat Sam in a production of *Bugsy Malone*. Work as an extra followed and he even got into the Italia Conti Academy, before being expelled for taking drugs. Russell had been well and truly bitten by the acting bug and won bit parts in the television shows *Mud* and *The Bill*, after which he got a place at the Drama Centre London. Unfortunately he was expelled again, this time for smashing a glass and stabbing himself in the chest and arms in response to a reaction to his performance. It was at this point that he decided comedy was his thing and briefly linked up with Karl Theobald, a friend from the Drama Centre, in Theobald and Brand on Ice.

Russell's first appearance of note was at the Hackney Empire in 2000, but other than that his life was a mess. He was a serious alcoholic and heroin addict, and was arrested eleven times over the course of his addiction, on occasion stripping naked at demos and fighting with the police. He was thrown out of Edinburgh's Gilded Ballroom for abusive behaviour and even introduced his drug dealer to Kylie Minogue, of all people. He was scoring drugs among the down-and-outs and his life had become completely shambolic. Meanwhile he was cutting a swathe through the female population, being branded Shagger of the Year no less than three times by the *Sun*, which went on to rename the award The Russell Brand Shagger of the Year Award!

It was in 2002 that Russell finally pulled himself together. His agent John Noel discovered Russell taking drugs in a bathroom during his Christmas party. John read him the riot act and that was that: Russell joined AA and NA – he still attends meetings to this day – and cleaned up his act. One thing he didn't abandon, however, was his womanizing – until he met Katy that is. Russell became a fully fledged sex addict, once even hiring a crew to help him find women. His girlfriends and companions included Kate Moss (a one-night stand that was seemingly instigated by her and which Russell credited with massively boosting his media profile), Teresa Palmer (an Australian actress who briefly seemed to be a contender to tame him), Georgina Baillie (Andrew Sachs' granddaughter, who warned that he would break Katy's heart), Holly Madison (Hugh Hefner's ex, who was his girlfriend during the filming of *Get Him to the Greek*) and Christy Peterson (who revealed that after sending her out shopping with his mum, Russell once had a threesome with a fan and a stripper).

Christy's account revealed why so many jaws hit the floor when he ended up with Katy, who clearly wouldn't tolerate such behaviour. 'Russell told me he loved me but he needed to have other women to remain sane,' Christy told the *News of the World*. 'He said it was a chemical imbalance in his brain – it was like a handicapped person needing a wheelchair. Russell gave me three options – leave, join in, or turn a blind eye. Stupidly I went for number three, which pretty much doomed our relationship. One Sunday he dragged me up to the bedroom, grabbed my arm and said, "I'm having an urge." I panicked and he said, "Christy, please join me with the other girls." But I just couldn't do that.

'I almost died one day when he beckoned me to the wardrobe and pulled out a bulging carrier bag. He told me to look inside and pulled out a load of sex toys. Some of them were so strange-looking, I had no idea what they even did. When I'd stopped laughing, I told him there was no way on earth he'd be using them on me. He called me a spoilsport.'

Then there was a woman called Catherine Coppin who showed off the love bites Russell had given her, Courtney Love – yes, that Courtney Love – Hannah Gregory-Soskin, Makosi Musambasi, a reality-TV show star, and, by his own account, many nights with numerous other partners, their names long forgotten, and on one occasion nine women in one night.

According to Russell, it wasn't all fun. 'When you have sex that often, by a law of averages you're likely to have boring sex,' he once said. 'But also, you do encounter a lot of intrigue, you learn about people's behaviour very quickly – the smells of people, the way they carry and present themselves. The fame and kind of will that I had meant that, instead of taking someone for a date and then going to the pictures and then calling them, I was able to go, "Let's do sex right now!"'

As his frankly exhausting personal life was developing, so, too, was his career. After that breakthrough at the Hackney Empire and performances in Edinburgh, Russell started to gain quite a reputation, in spite of his addictions, and once he'd beaten his problems he really began to flourish. In 2004, he performed a one-man show, Better Now, at the Edinburgh Festival, which was a brutally honest account of his heroin years. The next year he returned with Eroticised Humour, which he followed with the Shame tour. This was later immortalized on the DVD, *Russell Brand Live*.

By this time Russell had made the leap from cult figure to the mainstream, unsurprising considering that he's actually extremely funny. Adopting a camp persona and constantly referring to himself as a 'beta male' – something not entirely backed up by his rampant sex life – Russell would leap and prance about the stage, telling self-deprecating stories of more masculine men getting the better of him.

This, of course, just served to make the audience love him more. The accent was estuary, but his grasp of language belied a keen intellect: a university don would have been proud of the wordplay Russell engaged in, and his sense of the ridiculous shone through. Rake thin and invariably clad top to toe in black, with a wild exuberance of black hair and heavy designer stubble, Russell exuded charm. His language was as fruity as his reputation, but there was genuine wit on display, not just a stream of obscenity that the audience was supposed to find funny. Most of all, Russell had charisma, which explained why so many women fell for his charms.

Whole audiences fell for him, too, and Russell became ever more popular, with appearances at the 2006 Secret Policeman's Ball and, in 2007, the ultimate proof he'd made it: the Royal Variety Performance. More tours and DVDs followed and, in March 2009, a little while after his film work in America had begun, he decided to try out his comedy in the United States.

All the while, Russell had been steadily building up a career as a presenter, which might well have hastened the success of his film career later on. His earliest role as a presenter was in his drug-fuelled days, when he worked on MTV, presenting the Dancefloor Chart, touring night-clubs in Britain and Ibiza. This stint came to an abrupt end when he was fired for coming to work dressed as Osama bin Laden the day after the September 11 terrorist attacks – an early indication that Russell and presenting might prove a combustible combination. They weren't too keen on the fact that Russell brought his drug dealer to the MTV studios, either.

Despite his controversial nature, his presenting career lasted for quite a while. He starred in *RE:Brand*, a documentary taking a look at cultural taboos and therefore right up his street; *Big Brother's Eforum*, which turned into *Big Brother's Big Mouth*; various other *Big Brother*-related outings; a chat show called *1 Leicester Square*, which was shown on MTV and managed to attract the likes of Tom Cruise and Uma Thurman, and *The Russell Brand Show*.

Russell had shown himself to be pretty sharp-witted and was fast turning into an A-list star. He presented the 2006 NME Awards, during which Bob Geldof remarked, 'Russell Brand – what a cunt.'

'Really, it's no surprise,' replied Russell. 'Geldof's an expert on famine. He has after all been dining out on "I Don't Like Mondays" for thirty years.' More followed, including Comic Relief and various documentaries.

It was through his presenting work that Russell made his first mini-breakthrough in the United States. He was announced as the host of the 2008 MTV Video Music Awards, which caused raised eyebrows in some quarters, not only because many Americans had never heard of him, but because his performances were famous for being close to the bone. A tradition appears to have developed whereby British comedians go to American awards ceremonies and deliver speeches that insult half the audience and delight the rest, and Russell can claim to be at the vanguard of that movement.

'Please, America, elect Barack Obama,' he began. 'On behalf of the world.' Some people cheered; some didn't.

This was a Brit, after all, commenting on US politics. Matters didn't calm down when Russell called President Bush 'that retarded cowboy fellow' who 'wouldn't be trusted with scissors' in the UK, before moving on to the subject of himself. 'I'm famous in the United Kingdom,' he explained. 'My persona don't really work without fame. Without fame, this haircut could be mistaken for mental illness.'

The biggest female star of the evening was Britney Spears, who opened the show as part of her latest career revival; after a very turbulent period in her personal life, she appeared to be back on track. The night 'marked the launch of a very new Britney Spears era', commented Russell. It was, he said, 'The resurrection of Britney.'

And with that, it was anything goes. As the young stars of the *Twilight* films came on stage, a mystified Russell declared, 'These books are bloody popular, these "Twilight" books,' before poking fun at Levi Johnston, the then boyfriend of Sarah Palin's daughter Bristol: 'That is the safe sex message of all time. Use a condom or become a Republican!'

He then teased the Jonas Brothers – ironically, the children of a pastor – for wearing purity rings, the symbol of a vow not to have premarital sex, moving the *American Idol* star Jordin Sparks to comment, 'It's not bad to wear a promise ring because not everybody, guy or girl, wants to be a slut, OK?'

Later she was unabashed: 'It's his job to be funny and crack jokes, it was just a little much so I just decided to say something and I had no idea it was going to be such a big thing,' she said. 'Everybody is totally entitled to their opinions, that's what's so great about the world we live in, but sometimes it gets a little too much when you hear the same thing. For me sometimes it gets a little annoying.'

On the night itself Russell, while toning it down a bit, was unapologetic. 'A bit of sex occasionally never hurt anybody,' said Russell, a man who practised what he preached.

His remarks about the Jonas Brothers were guaranteed to make a big impact on an American audience, but the boys themselves responded with great courtesy: 'For us, it's cool to see that he recognizes we are gentlemen,' Nick, who at the time was only fifteen, said.

Kevin, who was then twenty, added, 'I think he focused on certain things and didn't move off of them. People's attention spans in America need more than that.'

'I think he did a good job,' said Nick. 'We saw him on Conan O'Brien and thought he was hilarious.'

'We had a lot of friends there and everybody's so nice. We had a good time,' said Kevin.

Various celebrities were, however, keen to stand up for the Jonas brothers, including Paris Hilton, of all people, who declared, 'I don't pick on them. That's something cool for a kid to keep, so don't pick on them for that.' And Katy's friend Perez Hilton also had something to say: 'I think those Jonas Brothers are good kids, and we shouldn't be making fun of them for promoting good values.'

Whatever your views, Russell made a splash — ratings

were up 20 per cent on the previous year and, in 2009, he was asked to host the awards again. The 2008 VMAs had done something else, too – they'd introduced Russell to Katy Perry, who won an award that night for Best New Artist with 'I Kissed A Girl'. Katy was still with Travis at the time, but an interview she gave to Scott Mills on Radio 1 certainly hinted at what was to come. 'Oh, I met Russell Brand [at the awards], who I'm in love with,' she said. 'I love him! He's so great. He's got the worst sense of humour in the best sense of the way.' Americans didn't really like it? asked Scott. 'No, we loved it!' Katie replied. 'I think it's such a hogwash. I got every single joke and it was like, if I could host an awards show, I would probably be as cruel as that . . .'

She was told it was dangerous to say she loved Russell Brand. 'Oh we all know . . . he's spreading his seed,' said Katy. 'Spreading the love. There'll be lots of little Brands.'

'You haven't, er . . .'

'No. Oh, no. We kissed once.'

'Oh really?'

'But it was for a movie.'

'You kiss him and then he wees over a balcony or something?'

'Something like that. There was a cameo and other people participated. We were at the VMAs and he asked if I'd do a cameo and I was like, sure! You're hilarious. Of course.'

'He's a nice man.'

'Yeah, he's a nice man.'

The love affair was yet to blossom, but the spark was clearly already there. From that moment on, Katy's love affair with Travis was doomed.

For Russell, too, the romantic die was cast, although he didn't know it yet. And still his profile continued to soar. As far back as 2002 he had started to revive his acting career, which had always been his first love, appearing in *Cruise of the Gods* and *White Teeth*. In 2005, viewers saw him in Ben Elton's *Blessed*, and 2007 produced parts in *Cold Blood*, playing an ex-con called Ally, and *The Abbey*, where he played a recovering crack addict called Terry.

Slowly, however, Russell was turning his mind to films. His first cinema role was in the 2006 film *Penelope*, but his first appearance of any real consequence was as Flash Harry in the 2007 remake of *St Trinian's*. Then came the real breakthrough, with spectacular reviews, in *Forgetting Sarah Marshall*. The character of Aldous Snow had originally been an author, but when Russell became involved it was changed to a rock star and it worked spectacularly well.

'In fairness, he excels,' wrote Chris Robert in *Uncut*. 'It helps that he's playing himself, pretty much, as conccited, promiscuous Brit-rocker Aldous. His band: Infant Sorrow. Their refrain: Sodomize Intolerance. He steals TV actress Sarah (*Veronica Mars* star Bell) from Peter (screenwriter Segel, our sensitive-loser). Peter is distraught. He weeps, drinks, shags inappropriately. Then he holidays in Hawaii. And who's in the same hotel? Sarah and Aldous, shagging inappropriately. With mostly hilarious consequences.

'Fortunately for Peter – and the feel-good factor – hotel employee Rachel (Kunis, *Family Guy*'s Meg, no less) is into him. Faces from kindred movies cameo, not least Paul Rudd's stoned surfer. With an acerbic sub-plot lampooning *CSI*, albeit with more penis and vagina gags, this is as smart as it is filthy.'

From that moment on, Russell's focus began to change, helped along by yet more controversy, again as a result of his presenting work, but this time on the radio. He'd had various radio shows since 2002 – he was fired from the first one after reading pornographic material live on air – but by 2006 he was very much in the mainstream with *The Russell Brand Show* on Radio 2. It seemed an oddly conservative dock for such a maverick, and so it was to prove when, in October 2008, with his film career already underway and American audiences starting to take notice of this strange new Brit, Russell self-destructed yet again.

The trouble began when he invited the equally maverick, but older and more experienced, broadcaster Jonathan Ross on to his show. The two of them rang the veteran actor Andrew Sachs, best known for his role as Manuel in *Fawlty Towers*, and left a series of vulgar messages on his answering machine. These concerned Georgina Baillie, Russell's ex, who also happened to be Andrew's granddaughter. The series of messages left Andrew in no doubt as to the nature of Georgina's relationship with Russell, and Russell and Jonathan egged each other on to ever greater levels of crudeness. In one of the biggest lapses of judgement ever to occur on the BBC, the episode was broadcast in full.

The exchange came about because Andrew was supposed to have been appearing on Russell's show, but failed to turn up. Russell informed his audience that Andrew hadn't shown up and that he was therefore planning to telephone him. However, Russell happily told his audience, Andrew was unaware of Russell's brief relationship with his granddaughter.

It turned out that Andrew wasn't in to take the phone call, so the duo decided to leave a message. It started off light-heartedly enough, with Jonathan chiding Russell for nearly calling Andrew by the name of his most famous creation, Manuel. Russell protested that he had the greatest respect for Andrew and his extended family, which Jonathan told him was a hint, and then it was Jonathan who started the ball rolling by informing Andrew of the relationship between Russell and Georgina, except in the crudest possible terms, using the 'F' word, after which Russell protested and Jonathan apologized.

Plainly forgetting that this was an elderly and much-respected actor, the pair then allowed matters to get totally out of hand. Egging each other on, they apologized to Andrew while repeating the misdemeanour. Russell then got wildly concerned that he would be contacted by Georgina's burlesque troupe, the Satanic Sluts – which it subsequently emerged Andrew hadn't known about – while Jonathan mused on the fact that most grandparents had an innocent image of their grandchildren, something that would now forever be destroyed. Tasteful it was not.

It seemed that matters could not get worse, but they did. The pair had by now hung up, but then they called Andrew a second time, with Russell offering to marry Georgina, with Jonathan as the page boy in a *Fawlty Towers*-themed wedding. Russell then mentioned that he'd worn a condom before hanging up again. With common sense long flown out of the window, they then rang Andrew for a third time. This time Russell sang a song of apology, but given that it was even more explicit about what had happened with Georgina, it didn't exactly help matters. Russell and Jonathan hung up and rang one last time – cue more apologies, more confessions and more loss of judgement. The exchange ended with Jonathan musing that no one could possibly be offended by what had gone on. He might have been being ironic, but he couldn't have been more wrong.

What made matters worse was that this wasn't even live. Though both men had clearly lost their heads and got carried away, the show was being recorded in advance, which meant that someone, somewhere could have prevented it being broadcast. Indeed, it later emerged that Jonathan Ross had voiced doubts about the wisdom of airing it and, ultimately, although he clung on longer – Ross did not, after all, have a burgeoning Hollywood career to turn to – he paid a higher price. A collective fit of insanity seemed to come over the BBC, however, and the show was broadcast.

Shortly afterwards the roof fell in. Record numbers of complaints were made after the story was picked up by a Sunday newspaper, and the BBC was eventually fined £150,000 for the broadcast, while Jonathan and Russell were both suspended from their various shows. Russell did the sensible thing and resigned shortly afterwards, but Jonathan unwisely hung on until, discredited, he had no option but to step down.

Rather more sadly, the furore caused a rift in the Sachs family. Andrew and his wife Melody did not know that their granddaughter Georgina was a burlesque dancer, going by the name of Voluptua, with a group called the Satanic Sluts, and were so shocked that they broke off contact. Meanwhile, the Controller of Radio 2, Lesley Douglas, resigned. Georgina said that she felt shocked and humiliated, even though both men publicly apologized to her at a later date, and the matter was such big news it was even raised in the House of Commons. To this day, it's talked of as an example of the BBC's laissez-faire behaviour and a shocking waste of licence payers' money.

Russell, though, had bigger fish to fry. After resigning and drawing a line under the matter – far more successfully than Jonathan Ross, it has to be said – he returned to the States, where some big movie roles were being lined up for him. He starred in Disney's *Bedtime Stories* alongside Adam Sandler, reunited with the old crew for *Get Him to the Greek* and even signed up for a remake of the famous Dudley Moore film *Arthur*.

The whole debacle was just another incident in Russell's

eventful life. At that point he seemed like a one-man stud operation, determined to bed every woman he came across. Only one woman would be able to tame him, and it wasn't going to be long before they got together . . .

A Star Rises

When Katy met Russell, she couldn't have been aware of his reputation for courting controversy and mayhem wherever he went, although on the back of the VMAs, she saw that he could cause a fuss when he was in the mood. Then again, Katy wasn't unaccustomed to controversy herself, given the nature and title of her first two singles.

No matter how much she'd liked Russell, though, there was no time to dwell on him: there was work to be done. It had taken a great deal of effort to get to where she was, and she had no intention of stopping now. In 2008 she appeared in the Warped Tour, a touring festival of music and extreme sports that Gym Class Heroes were also taking part in.

According to Katy, her parents were now completely happy with what she was doing, and as interest about her background intensified, she was only too happy to talk about her happy upbringing. 'My parents are definitely supportive and happy for my success,' she told *The Times*. 'I think if they did it their way, then maybe I wouldn't be singing a song with this subject matter, but I'm an adult, I make my own decisions now. It was more like, Katy's always had something to say, now she's saying . . . this. I'm happy with where I came from. I love my family, and I like my upbringing. I think it was pure.'

It had certainly protected her against some of show-business's worst excesses, while giving her the self-confidence to tame a great ladies' man like Russell Brand. Her remarks were also a sign that Katy was becoming increasingly protective of her parents. They inhabited a different world from hers, and Katy was aware that this made them the object of some less-than-kind remarks from some quarters, which angered her and made her quick to defend them.

Katy's success was beginning to arouse resentment in some quarters, though. According to Perez Hilton who, whilst a supporter of Katy, was inclined to stir things up a little, other female artists of her age were feeling fed up. In June 2008, he reported that Lily Allen was beginning to feel a little cheesed off: 'And the battle is on!' he blogged. 'It's hard to stay on top in the music industry. Just ask Lily Allen! Lily used to be Capitol Records' "golden girl", but lately she's been slipping. She's known these days more for being a tragic train wreck than a musician. She knows it too. That must hurt! And now it seems she's been replaced. Replaced by none other than a Perez fav, Katy Perry, which we first introduced you to last year . . .

'Well, according to reports, a music industry insider has said, "Lily Allen is peeved at Capitol. She feels like they've shoved her aside to focus all their energies on their new girl of the moment, Katy Perry." But the real insult, according to the source, came when the label "replaced a photo of Lily Allen with one of Katy Perry" in its office main lobby. Ha ha ha ha!!!!!

'Lily is starting to look like washed-up goods. The only thing that can save Allen now is if she makes a good sophomore album! But, from what we're hearing, Lily's new material s-u-c-k-s.'

Initially, Lily responded with some dignity, replying via a blog on MySpace. 'I don't know why this has annoyed me so much,' she began. 'If I'm honest, it's probably because part of it is true, these days I am more known for being a train wreck than a musician, and it does hurt. I've been working really hard on my new record; I don't think it sucks by the way. I haven't released a record for two years, so it's totally understandable that people don't write about my music anymore, however it's not fair to say that I'm washed up and it's not fair to make up these feuds between people. Not everyone's lives are fuelled by egos and jealousy, mine is certainly not.

'This is not meant in any way [sic] but I'd never heard of Katy Perry before I came here a few days ago, I didn't even know she was on Capitol, who by the way are not my label. I am signed to Regal Records in the UK and Capitol distributes my records here in America. I don't feel like I've been shoved aside for anyone, I haven't got a record out yet, so why would anyone be focusing their energies on me when there's nothing to work on!

'I have never been a "golden girl" and I think I visited Capitol's office in New York once, about a year and a half ago. I very much doubt they had a picture of me in their lobby. The point I'm trying to make is these stories are just not true. If the word reportedly exists in a story it means that it's pretty much a lie, it means they can't prove what they're writing and their [sic] just covering their backs. Perez doesn't even do this he just writes things that aren't true with no shame about it, and it's sad.

'I read these posts on his website about anti-bullying campaigns and all these good causes, and while I used to enjoy reading his site it seems to me that recently he has become what he hates so much, a bully. He bullies young, successful females; people usually bully people they're jealous of so I'll let you come to your own conclusion on that one.'

Perez, who's not known for taking these things lying down, replied, 'In her blog rant from earlier today, Lily Allen spread a bunch of lies, most of which are easily debunked. Claims the British train wreck, "And this is not meant in any way [to be mean] but I'd never heard of Katy Perry before I came here [to L.A.] a few days ago, I didn't even know she was on Capitol." Uhmm, liar!'

At first, Katy gave the impression that she didn't realize how the row had broken out. Apart from anything else, she was working extremely hard, giving interviews, touring, working on her next projects and giving every sign of being totally in charge of her career. Many pop stars are given little say in how they are presented to the wider public, but Katy, having worked so hard to get where she was, wasn't going to relinquish control. 'I have people who are working with me who know exactly how I want to be portrayed, and my vision,' she told *The Times*. 'You know, me – Katy Perry – very sassy, cheeky, fun, cute, sexy and smart.'

This kind of breeziness went down very well with the public, and she was becoming well liked – in most quarters – because of a combination of charm, her unwillingness to take herself too seriously and sheer hard work. The more people met her, the more they discovered that, far from being a brazen hussy who went around shocking people with her outrageous behaviour, she was what would once have been known as a 'nice girl', someone who's polite, well-mannered and doesn't sleep around. Katy still gamely told everyone that yes, she had kissed a girl, but as often as not even that came across as innocent. She'd kissed a girl, yes, but in a manner more reminiscent of slumber parties than the debauchery of an orgy.

Meanwhile preparations were underway for Katy's next single, 'Hot N Cold'. Her charm continued to become more apparent: far from the slanging matches she inadvertently got involved in, she was full of praise for her fellow stars. 'I saw Leona at the MTV awards in LA and was blown away,' she gushed at one point. 'She is absolutely beautiful and has an amazing voice. Wow. I'm quite a fan!' That was the way to make friends and influence people, a fact that Katy only rarely forgot.

Katy was beginning to perform in the UK, too, albeit on a smaller scale than in the US. Her London debut was at a pub called the Water Rats. Sporting minuscule black shorts and a red top, she blasted out 'I Kissed A Girl' to an ecstatic crowd. The strategy had been carefully thought out: no one was certain that Katy could fill a larger venue in the UK – although she probably could have done – but by placing her in a smaller one, they not only ensured it was a sell-out, but that there were hordes of ecstatic fans crowding outside, too. All of this helped to promote that all-important buzz. On the whole the critics loved it, pointing out that Katy was a far more polished performer than the acts that usually appeared in the pub. She was clearly on her way to becoming an international star.

'With eyelashes the size of awnings and a plunging red and black top, she mugged glamorously in much the same way women in 1950s magazine ads did when posing beside Frigidaires,' wrote Pete Paphides in a perceptive review in *The Times*. 'The longer she and her band played, the clearer it became that the sexually ambiguous hit song that smoothed her passage to fame is something of an aberration.

'The paradox of Katy Perry is that – deliberately or otherwise – her image conforms to a heterosexual man's idea of sexiness.' He was less complimentary about the rest of the concert, however, pointing out that not all the numbers were up to the standards of her hit single.

Rose Dennen of the *Daily Telegraph* enjoyed the show, too. 'Perry's *Carry On* film salaciousness and playful seaside-postcard get-ups have proved extremely appealing,' she wrote. 'She is something of an Amy Winehouse for the tweens, but her music has drawn an unlikely crowd of twentysomethings to this show. The opening song, "Fingerprints", is a bouncing pop track that owes a lot to Gwen Stefani's first band No Doubt, in its girls-against-the-boys lyrics and punching-the-air bravado. The rest of the set sees her switch between toy-boy flirtations and coy naivety which gives the impression that she's a little confused at the fact that her "Kitty Kat Fan Club" isn't entirely made up of teenagers.'

Katy was to prove considerably more than a one-hit wonder, but at this stage people were only interested in 'I Kissed A Girl' and, as many performers before her have done, she soon began – in the nicest way possible – to tire of the number that had served her so well thus far.

'The song follows me around wherever I am in the world, it's all people wanna hear,' she told the *Daily Star*. 'But I can't get too sick of it as it's paying for my grand-children's college tuition. Maybe in three years I'll retire it or something. It's funny in certain situations – like when you walk into the grocery store and they're playing it and then I get in my car and it's on the radio. I'm like, "Please. I get it."'

But revenge was sweet. Katy might have been extremely good-natured, but even she couldn't fail to feel a smidgeon of satisfaction at how the record labels who'd dumped her had been proved so wrong. 'I call the music industry "musical chairs",' she said. 'It's always changing, signing people, letting important artists go. I wasn't really under-stood at the time but I probably didn't understand myself either back then. It's funny because, before I joined EMI, I was at Columbia. Within a year, that label had let go of me, the Jonas Brothers, OneRepublic and Ne-Yo, so some-body probably got fired.' It was the nearest she'd come – so far – to a bitchy remark.

Katy's utter delight at what was happening to her was infectious: she could hardly believe she was so popular, so successful and that so many people wanted to see her. Per-haps as a result of all the disappointment she'd experienced earlier in her career, though, she didn't let it go to her head. She didn't become grand, ignore those who were less suc-cessful, or forget her background, and she appeared willing to draw everyone into her realm. The way her life had sped up was astonishing. Young and energetic, she could hardly believe how far and how fast she'd come, and she wasn't just making the most of it, she was loving it.

'I feel like I've been on tour since it's been happening, which is awesome,' she told the *Sun*. 'I get to see the crowds grow and people get more excited. One girl fainted. It was crazy. I was like, "Chill out! It's just me!" This morning I was in Milan and a couple of mornings before that I was in Germany and London and Paris, I'm zig-zagging all over Europe. Then, for like 17 days, I'm in Australia, New Mexico and Japan. It's incredibly hectic but there are no complaints. The perks are fucking amazing and I'm doing what I always wanted to do. I'm gonna be playing on *Jools Holland* tonight and then I'll have like an hour and a half of downtime, I just wanna go out and bop around.'

In the same interview she was asked what she thought of Russell Brand: 'He's hot in person,' said Katy. 'I appreci-

'California Gurl'

In demand all over the world

On stage at Vienna's Life Ball, performing to a high-profile audience that included Bill Clinton and Pamela Anderson

At the Hurricane Festival in Germany

Below: Performing on Italian *X Factor*

It's official. Good girl Katy leaves Russell Brand's house in London after spending the night there in October 2009. The unlikely couple made headlines when Brand admitted they were dating

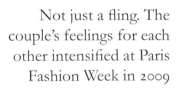

Not just a fling. The couple's feelings for each other intensified at Paris Fashion Week in 2009

Katy has appeared in *FHM*'s 100 Sexiest Women poll twice

The happy couple at an awards ceremony after-party in LA one month after their lavish wedding ceremony in India

There were incredulous responses to the news that Lothario Russell Brand had married. His notorious sexual appetite led to the *Sun* newspaper renaming their annual awards 'The Russell Brand Shagger of the Year Award' after he won it three years in a row

Katy and Russell's devotion to one another is obvious, and both have expressed their desire to start a family

Enjoying a sky-high profile, Katy was invited to guest judge *American Idol* with Kara DioGuardi and Simon Cowell

Showing off her inner child – Katy at the 2010 Nickelodeon Kids' Choice Awards

Katy's parents, Mary and Keith Hudson, who provided the grounded Christian upbringing that has helped to keep Katy level-headed

With her beloved grandmother

Dressing up with good friend Perez Hilton

Best friend Rihanna, who is rumoured to disapprove of Russell and therefore declined the invitation to their wedding in 2010

The girl's done good – a multi-award-winning pop princess and a fully fledged star

ate his kind of fucked up sense of humour, he's hilarious.'
Clearly Russell had made a big impression.

'Hot N Cold' had now been released, and slowly it
began to rise up the charts. Meanwhile the impact of her
first hit was still being felt. The comedian Katy Brand (no
relation) announced plans to do a spoof, changing the lyrics
from, 'I kissed a girl and I liked it,' to, 'I kissed a girl and I
faked it.' Katy P was in good company, though, as other
targets of Katy Brand's humour included Lily Allen and
Amy Winehouse.

Katy's good-humoured approach to life continued:
there was a mini-scene at MTV's Latin America Awards in
Guadalajara, Mexico, in October 2008, when a stunt went
wrong. Katy dived into a giant cake at an awards party, but
slipped on the icing, fell, grabbed a bandmate to try to
stop herself but hit the ground anyway, covered in cream,
cake and icing sugar. Unlike some artistes, who would have
created havoc, Katy just laughed it off.

However, she did occasionally get it wrong, such as
when she sparked outrage by posing with a flick knife for
a publicity photo. The shot didn't go down well in Britain,
where teenage stabbings were getting out of control. Singing about kissing girls could be laughed off; this could not.
Campaigners called her 'out of her mind', and with awful
timing Joey Lappin, a sixteen-year-old cadet, was knifed to
death in Liverpool around the time the photo came out.

For a time the episode threatened to derail Katy's UK
career. The father of Damilola Taylor, a young boy who
was stabbed to death in a particularly ugly killing in south

London in 2000, was appalled, and anti-violence campaigners were disgusted by the message the picture sent out. Most of all, it was so un-Katy. The clean-living pastor's daughter who dressed up like a 1950s teenager was emphatically not the sort of girl to go around carrying knives: it didn't fit with her image and it didn't match her character, either. If it was an attempt to recast her as an 'edgy' performer, then that, too, was a mistake, because Katy was receiving so much positive publicity she didn't need to be reinvented. The incident refused to blow over, though, and outrage continued on all sides until it became apparent that someone was going to have to act to limit the damage.

Matters got so bad that Katy's spokesman was forced to broadcast a statement on MTV: 'Katy Perry is against all violence,' he said. 'The photo in question was taken in 2005 and is in no way related to the current events in the UK.' It was a salutary reminder that being in the public eye came with a certain amount of responsibility: Katy couldn't laugh off potentially controversial actions by being playful or attempting to be cool. In the end she tried to put the episode behind her by posting a similar picture, but this time with her licking a spoon. 'But I DO condone eating ice cream with a very large spoon,' the caption read.

She later admitted that the controversy had taken its toll. 'I was misrepresented because it was taken three or four years ago,' she said just before hosting the MTV European Music Awards in Liverpool. 'It wasn't something I was trying to hide. I'm a very open book kind of

girl. Of course I'm a pop girl and I wanna make people happy so it hurt me to be connected to something that is really a big deal for you guys in the UK right now. I don't care if people make fun of me, I don't care if they trash my record, but when I'm put into that kind of position I feel helpless.'

That comment seemed to do the trick and Katy was finally allowed to get on with her life – and what a life it was turning into. Her status at the MTV Awards – presenting, performing and being nominated – was indicative of how successful she'd become, so much so that the idea of Katy performing in a London pub now seemed ludicrous. Twelve dress changes were planned for the awards ceremony – none accessorized with a knife! – and the fact that she'd been officially forgiven became apparent when she was pictured goosing a tall Liverpudlian, prompting a great deal of affectionate press coverage. Her career was back on track.

On the night of the awards, Katy was one of the brightest stars, although she was once again forced to share the limelight with Britney Spears, whose comeback was confirmed when she won two awards. Katy and her many costume changes, including a tribute to the newly elected President Obama when she sported his image made out of sequins, certainly kept her in the spotlight. She opened the awards with 'I Kissed A Girl', riding on a huge cherry chapstick and surrounded by cheerleaders. 'I've seen bigger,' purred Katy as she stroked the giant chapstick, then she waved to Travis: 'Hi, baby.' Katy picked up a gong for

best new act, beating Miley Cyrus and the Jonas Brothers in the process. Travis, meanwhile, had had Katy's name tattooed on his wedding ring finger – a romantic gesture that was ultimately to no avail.

That night Travis had eyes only for Katy, telling everyone how sexy it was to see her hosting the show, while Katy was livid when, during the after-show party at Liverpool's Circo club, women surrounded him to inspect his piercings and tattoos. 'Why don't you whores just piss off?' she snarled, showing a slightly less lovable side than the world was used to seeing. Katy was learning about another, less appealing aspect of showbusiness: the men get surrounded by extremely predatory girls. Not that Katy went unappreciated: 'She looked pretty good in the flesh,' said Lemar. 'Better than I thought.'

It seemed that Britain was taking Katy to its heart and Katy was just as effusive in return. She picked up on all things British and delighted her hosts with her enthusiasm, expressing a wish to present *Antiques Roadshow*, of all things: 'Any girl knows there is no better feeling than getting a great bargain,' she told the *Sun*. 'I love it! It's the thrill, the chase and the chance to get something great. So many people have no idea what it is they are just giving away. I'll put the hair under a cap and put on a pair of sunglasses and rarely get noticed when I am on the searches. I am like a pirate or a scavenger ready to swoop when I see something worthwhile. When I was a kid my dad would wake me up every Saturday morning and we'd go out

looking for stuff. Plus my mum was an antiques dealer in London, so I guess some of it trickled down to me.'

The idea of Katy on the *Antiques Roadshow* was a novel one, but it was just another example of her winning charm. Everything British seemed to appeal: she let it be known that she loved British comedy and was buying box sets of *Gavin & Stacey* and *Little Britain*, as well as one, interestingly enough, by Russell Brand. The rest of the world was also wising up to her appeal, and Katy was inundated with clothes from fashion designers, all of them aware of the huge boost their business would get if Katy was seen wearing their clothes in public. On the down side, Katy had to put up with plenty of gossip, too. One often repeated rumour was that she'd had a breast enhancement: 'I'd never spend money on fake boobs,' said Katy wearily. 'Shoes, a handbag, maybe. But plastic tits? No way.' To illustrate the point, she donated a plaster cast of her embonpoint (32DD) to be sold for charity on eBay.

Her easy charm and occasionally hair-raising pro-nouncements had the public eating out of her hand, but it wasn't quite as spontaneous as it looked. A lot of money had gone into marketing Katy, and the record company wanted to make sure it had a hit. Asked if she deliberately courted controversy, Katie replied, 'No, but it was a delib-erate strategy to be charismatic. I'm not sitting over a witches' brew saying, "What can I do to piss off the people now?" I've just always been quite frank and never had that filter from my brain to my mouth. Some people in this

business are very controlled. There's guys in suits moving puppet strings, so really they don't have any personality of their own.' The record company encouraged this strategy. They knew that Katy was fresh and charming and that their best policy was simply to let her true self shine through. Ironically, it was the very quality that her friend, music PR Mandy Collinger-Parsons, had highlighted as being a problem for the younger Katy, but now it was working to her benefit.

Travis continued to be as besotted as ever, and it was now that he started talking about the difficult times he'd had in the past and how Katy had helped him out of it. Her resilience, combined with the fact that she wasn't given to darkness and melancholy – nor, indeed, to drug use – made her the perfect person to help shift his despair. 'There was this really, really dark point about two years ago where I just hit rock bottom . . . and I called Katy who was in LA at the time and said to her, "Do you mind coming out and keeping me company, I'm not in a good state of mind right now,"' he told the *Daily Mirror*. 'And I honestly think had she not come – I really don't think I would be here right now. Without even talking, she just listened. I truly believe that saved my life.' Even so, their relationship was nearing its end. Katy and Russell had met, and it was only a matter of time before they became a couple.

The feud with Lily Allen had gone quiet over the past few months, but in December 2008 Lily revealed that the spat had escalated: 'When I met her I was bit frosty with her because someone asked her to describe herself,' she

said during a visit to Capital FM in London. 'She's like, "Aha, I'm like a fatter version of Amy Winehouse and a skinnier version of Lily Allen!" It's like, you're not English and you don't write your own songs, shut up!'

Lily then got cattier: 'I think she's got a great production team,' Lily said in the run-up to these acid remarks. 'I happen to know for a fact that she was an American version of me. She was signed by my label in America as, "We need to find something controversial and kooky like Lily Allen." And then they found her. ["I Kissed A Girl"'s] lyrics and stuff are a bit crass. I think it's good for what it is, but don't read too much into it because, pop music, who cares!?'

Katy was very embarrassed. She was still a relative newcomer, and she didn't want to get a reputation for being an arrogant little brat. 'Yeah, I made a joke about [that] earlier this year,' Perry said at the taping of Fuse's *The Good, the Bad & the Britney*. 'I was just kind of joking and trying to be funny. I didn't mean anything by it. Comedians are not necessarily to be taken super seriously.' She was polite, too: 'We sound different,' she said. 'She's in a league of her own.'

Lily refused to be won over, though. 'I have Katy Perry's number, someone did me a favour,' she proclaimed. 'I'm just waiting for her to open her mouth one more time then it hits Facebook.'

It must be said that Lily had form when it came to picking fights. She'd called Cheryl Cole a 'stupid bitch', said Madonna 'might have meant something once', and mused

that Kate Moss was 'not a role model but a clothes horse'. She excelled herself at an awards ceremony talking to Elton John: 'Fuck off, Elton,' she said. 'I'm forty years younger than you. I have my whole life ahead of me.' Tact is not one of Lily's strong points.

Even so, Katy was clearly not only a hugely talented singer, but a rival. She tried to rise above it all, giving an interview to the *News of the World* in which Lily was very pointedly not mentioned. 'I say what I think,' she said. 'I'm a real person, not some manufactured pop tart who's afraid to step out of the hotel room. I am flawed. I swear, I have the occasional cocktail, I pick my nose and I fart. I'm not running for any presidential campaign at the moment. I'm a sassy girl. My parents know I've always had a wild streak, so they're not shocked. They also know I have a good head on my shoulders. I've tried different things in my life and I have been lost, but I don't think I'm lost right now.'

She was spot on there. Despite the feud with Lily, which in any case simmered down after that, 2008 had been Katy's year. Year-end round-ups were beginning to appear, and Katy featured on just about all of them – or those that related to the entertainment industry at least. She had been a smash hit sensation all across the globe. As attention-seeking as the titles of her first two singles had been, they were not the only reasons Katy stood out from the crowd. It was the freshness of her personality that made her so appealing; the fact that she wasn't some manufactured pop songstress but the real thing, someone who'd had to strug-

gle to succeed, but who had eventually got through on the back of her talent.

The way Katy handled herself had come a long way, too. Long gone were the days when she would burp during interviews – although she maintained the iconoclastic quality from those early days – and indulge in long rambling monologues on stage. It wasn't an accident: she had been extensively trained over the years to contain herself and keep it professional on stage. Thankfully, though, she still had the same raw talent that had been spotted years earlier.

Now that Katy's professional life was in place; her personal life was about to follow. The end of 2008 marked the end – for the first time at least – of her relationship with Travis, and given how often he'd declared his love for Katy, it was easy to work out who wanted a way out. Meanwhile, Katy and Russell kept dropping one another's names in interviews, so there was clearly an attraction on both sides.

That didn't stop it taking everyone by surprise when Katy and Russell did finally get together. The secret was out that Katy was nothing like the raunchy figure she was portrayed as. In fact, she was a good girl whose only vice appeared to be the odd cocktail, who was vehemently anti-drugs and who expected her boyfriends to treat her with respect. Russell, on the other hand, was a world-famous Lothario. However, what most onlookers didn't realize was that beneath Russell's penchant for mischief and aptitude for troublemaking lay a genuinely nice man. Unlike Katy,

his childhood had been a troubled one, and a great deal of his flamboyant image and over-the-top behaviour was designed as a barrier to keep the world at bay. So although the pair seemed an odd match, he and Katy considered one another soul mates.

The Lady is a Vamp

Katy had had quite a year and she rounded it off in style by performing at midnight at the Gridlock New Year party at Paramount Studios. Dressed in a tight-fitting chemise she brought the house down once more. A star really had been born.

Meanwhile 'Hot N Cold', Katy's third single from her debut album, was performing very creditably indeed, proving that she was no one-hit wonder, while she prepared to embark on her first proper global tour, the Hello Katy tour. Marriage appeared to be on Katy's mind, too, in the video for 'Hot N Cold', where she's featured dressed as a bride about to exchange vows at the altar before the groom (played by Alexander Rodriguez) flees. Katy chases after him and much running around is done until it becomes clear that this was just his fantasy and the two say, 'I do' and skip off down the aisle. The song was said to have been inspired by Travis.

'Hot N Cold', written by Dr Luke, Max Martin and Katy, was generally well received by the critics, with *Blender* calling it a 'spunky, climate-controlled kiss-off', and it got plenty of coverage. Katy sang it at the Liverpool MTV Awards, on the American Top 40 radio show and on the first YouTube Live in 2008. She sang it in Simlish for the

soundtrack of *Sims 2: Apartment Life* and a mixed version was released for play in the iPhone OS game *Tap Tap Revenge*. It was nominated for a Grammy in the Best Female Pop Vocal Performance category, although in the end the winner was 'Halo' by Beyoncé. In 2010, Katy was to sing a version with Elmo for *Sesame Street*, which made it on to YouTube, but not *Sesame Street* itself, as Katy's clothing was deemed too revealing. 'In light of the feedback we've received on the Katy Perry music video ... we have decided we will not air the segment on the television broadcast of *Sesame Street*, which is aimed at preschoolers,' the Sesame Workshop announced. 'Katy Perry fans will still be able to view the video on YouTube.' Katy replied by appearing on *Saturday Night Live* wearing a red Elmo T-shirt, slashed to reveal why the original video had been banned. 'How do you respond otherwise?' she told *Harper's Bazaar*.

Ultimately, the song did even better than 'I Kissed A Girl', becoming Katy's first No 1 on both the Mainstream Top 40 and Adult Top 40 US charts and reaching No 4 in the UK. It also did well throughout Europe and Australia, clocking up No 1 positions in, amongst others, Austria, Canada, the Czech Republic, Denmark, Germany, Norway, Slovakia, Belgium, Finland, France, Hungary, the Netherlands, Switzerland and Romania. Various cover versions followed: the Atlanta-based rock band Woe Is Me put it on the compilation album *Punk Goes Pop*, Kid British sang it on iTunes Live: London Festival '09, The Chipettes sang it for the movie *Alvin and the Chipmunks*, Brazilian

girlband Valkyrias performed it on their Radio VKS tour and rockabilly cover band The Baseballs featured it on their debut album, *Strike*.

The song received a lot of coverage elsewhere, too. It was used to promote the Australian soap opera *Out of the Blue*, as the theme music for *MasterChef Australia*, during the opening sequence for the 2009 film *The Ugly Truth* starring Katherine Heigl and Gerard Butler and in the trailer for the film *The Proposal* starring Sandra Bullock and Ryan Reynolds. It was played on the TV show *Ghost Whisperer*, in *American Pie Presents: The Book of Love*, Mohamed sang it in the Danish version of *The X Factor* and it was sung by schoolboys at the beginning of an episode of *This American Life*. The song had well and truly entered popular culture, establishing Katy as a force to be reckoned with, both in the United States and overseas. It was also becoming apparent that Katy's success was translating into substantial wealth: the days when her cheques bounced and her cars were repossessed were long gone.

Although Katy was a considerably more polished performer than she had been in the early days, with a lot more foresight and planning about what she was doing and where her career was going, she still stood out from the crowd of bland popettes, as she actually had something to say for herself. And although she was perceptive about that quality, what she didn't seem to appreciate was quite how charming she was.

'The way my mind works isn't the normal, vanilla, bland idea,' she said in an interview with the *Scotsman*, which

showed a degree of self-knowledge without, perhaps, understanding quite how likeable she appeared to be. 'I've always been kind of unfiltered my whole life, not only in my songwriting but my friendships, my relationships. I think I just kind of say things, sometimes, that people have thought but never really had the balls to say. I think sometimes people are surprised that there is a girl that's in pop music that's just saying it like it is, because you're so used to these more controlled pop girls and Disney people. I think that, being a songwriter, you've got to tell good stories, and I tell all the colours of the rainbow, not just the pink ones.' That was true to some extent, even though Katy's image was still pretty bubblegum.

There was another track on the album *One of the Boys* that could well have been inspired by Travis, and that was her next (and worst-performing) single. 'Thinking Of You' was about a break-up: 'I touched it, I was burned'. 'It's probably the song on the record that means the most to me,' Katy told the *Scotsman*. 'I think it's me at my most vulnerable, I guess. The singles so far have only [shown], like, the middle-finger-to-the-boyfriend side of me or the more aggressive sides of me, and really I am a woman – I feel a range of emotions.'

She might have liked the single, but the record-buying public didn't. Indeed, it was to be a salutary reminder that not everything Katy touched turned to gold, and in truth it was something of a disappointment. It was penned by Katy alone, and was her first single since 'Ur So Gay' not

to have been produced by Dr Luke – this time the man in charge was Butch Walker. It did, however, do well in Brazil and Portugal, partly because it was on the soundtrack to a Brazilian television series called *India, A Love Story*.

In the all-important US, however, it only got to No 29, while in Canada it peaked at 34, in Ireland at 38 and in the UK at 27. Matters weren't helped by the video. Just as Travis had made a variety of videos for 'Cupid's Choke-hold', so Katy did the same here. An early version, which made it onto YouTube but was never commercially released, featured a variety of different rooms, including a white one with spilled red wine (which seemed to suggest blood), a dark one and a cloudy one. The camera flashed backwards and forwards between various versions of Katy, one in which she seemed to be reflecting on the past, and one in which she seemed to regret past actions. At the end of the video it's revealed that Katy had stabbed a man in the back in the white room. Katy was quick to claim that it was never intended for commercial release and that it had been 'made by a friend'.

The second video was a different proposition altogether. Featuring Matt Dallas and Anderson Davis and directed by the film-maker Melina Matsoukas, it told the story of a young woman whose first love is killed in France during the Second World War, and whose second lover proves to be a less-than-adequate replacement. It was a success on YouTube, if nothing else, with over 18 million hits to date. Meanwhile, the song itself was covered by the Jonas Brothers at the Live Lounge.

Katy's heavy workload at least took her mind off the split with Travis, which was beginning to get rather ugly, and would only become more painful and drawn out. As well as the comments posted in the previous chapter, Travis blogged another rant clearly aimed at his ex: 'My friends always tell me how I'm lucky to possess the best-looking girl in the whole US. But every time you scream, you blow your finesse. Yo, sweetheart, you better take a hint. I say it now like I said it before. I'm lookin' at the front door . . .'

At the time, it was widely assumed that it was Travis, not Katy, who was behind the split, but in reality a third party had entered the equation. The rest of Gym Class Heroes professed themselves to be pleased about it: 'People saw Travis dating Katy Perry and that's all they wanted to talk about,' said Matt McGinley, rather gracelessly. 'After we've slaved for three months writing this new record, we want everyone to hear it – not talk about gossip.' Some chance. Katy was fast heading for A-list status and that meant that everything she did and said became subjects of global fascination. If truth be told, she had outgrown Travis. She needed a man who enjoyed the same level of success, and that just wasn't the case here.

Katy had a brief holiday with her parents, which gave her time to think about what she wanted to happen next. It helped her to be with them, and they, in turn, enjoyed celebrating their daughter's success. 'My family and I are very close,' Katy told the *Mail on Sunday*. 'My parents can't believe that finally, after all this time of them depositing

money in my account just to get along and have groceries, that there's actually something coming of it.'

There certainly was, although there was the odd embarrassment along the way, too. In January 2009, Katy attended the NRJ Music Awards in Cannes, France's top music awards ceremony, where she was awarded the trophy for Best International Song, before the organizers realized there had been a mistake and it was meant to go to Rihanna for 'Disturbia'. She did, however, get the gong for Best International Album for *One of the Boys*.

As preparations for the tour continued, Katy revealed that the meticulous planning that had gone into getting her this far was still very much in evidence. She had made the breakthrough, now she needed to sustain her career. Nothing is more fickle than the music industry, so Katy started working with a man who had already collaborated with the most successful female singer of them all: Madonna.

'I have the guy who creates stages for Madonna working on this tour,' Katy told Billboard. 'I'm indulging my obsession with fruit and cats and designing all different outfits. All the big pop girls come across as being so scared [sic] and so distant. I understand diva-ness, but I cultivate an image as the pop star next door. You need to have some mystery and some privacy, and there are parts of me that I hold back. But, at the same time, I love meeting people.' It was exactly this mixture of starriness and accessibility that made Katy so popular.

There was some teasing about the reference to fruit,

but Katy did indeed utilize it in the tour. One poster had her in a little pink retro sundress, holding up a large slice of watermelon. Previously she had jumped on the stage out of a giant banana, and that banana was going to appear over and over again in the work she did. She was to appear at the Grammys, complete with banana, something that appeared to take even her aback: 'Really?! I can descend from the ceiling in a banana into a clear fruit bowl of androgynous dancers?' she asked when the organizers said yes. Of course she sang 'I Kissed A Girl' – no other number could quite compete with that one in the public mind – although she didn't actually win anything on the night. Katy had more success at the Brits in February, scooping the gong for International Female Solo Artist and, as usual, wearing a cute little outfit, this time made of rubber. The show that night, however, was stolen by Lady Gaga, the next massive female solo act to have broken through.

Katy's tour was going to be a major undertaking in what would turn out to be a very busy year: there would be a stint around North America, followed by a European leg, followed by another US leg in order to consolidate the position she had attained. She also began to branch out into other areas, writing a song called 'I Do Not Hook Up' for Kelly Clarkson, and by doing so Katy showed that she was able to chime in with other artists' modes of thought, too: 'It's almost like I wrote the song because it sounds so like me,' Kelly said.

In the wake of her split with Travis, Katy initially said she intended to be celibate for a year, though she retracted the comment pretty quickly. Who was the new lucky man going to be? Every man she was pictured with became a possible boyfriend, among them Benji Madden, Paris Hilton's ex. When Katy appeared on Rick Edwards' T4 special, she was subjected to a real grilling: 'You don't have a crush on me, do you?' purred Katy. 'Let's get down and dirty.' More than one viewer commented on the sparks that flew between the pair. Josh Groban was the next man to be named as her boyfriend, although he denied it, but no one seemed to have cottoned on to who would be the next man to win her heart.

Over in Europe, more specifically the UK, Katy was garnering terrific reviews. After a performance at the Manchester Academy, Kim Dawson wrote in the *Daily Star*, 'It's hard to imagine any other chart-topper bounding onstage to "Killer Queen", or dressed as Dorothy from Oz with giant inflatable cats and strawberries to play with. Whether jabbering about puking up Smurfs or even actually singing a song, the irrepressible Californian could do no wrong . . .

'After a swift costume change into the sexiest, tightest, most biteable catsuit ever seen – complete with tail and ears – Katy's encore was appropriately Queen's "Don't Stop Me Now" and the inevitable but brilliant "I Kissed A Girl".

'Ridiculous, camp, overblown, hot and basically everything good pop should be.'

All of this success meant that Katy was becoming bankable in other ways as well. Her old friends in The Matrix had been watching her ascent up the chart and realized that they, too, had an album featuring her work. While they had focused on their work as producers in the intervening years they had temporarily parted ways with their manager, but they were all together again now, and for some time there had been talk of bringing out the long forgotten disc they'd recorded with Katy. Columbia Records hadn't been interested in retaining the rights (this was pre-'I Kissed A Girl'), so The Matrix's own record label, Let's Hear It Records, bought the rights from them.

Initially there had been talk about releasing the disc in 2008, but when Katy was asked about it she wasn't keen, believing that she wasn't firmly enough established at that stage, and asking them to hold back. They did, but by early 2009 it became clear that they were sitting on a goldmine, so they decided to release it. The ensuing publicity did nothing to hurt Katy's image; instead it reminded everyone of the fact that she'd had a long hard slog to the top. The album was called *The Matrix* and it had a good reception, with many commentators recognizing Katy's star quality.

It was certainly interesting to compare the current Katy with the younger version. Also featuring the British singer Adam Longlands, the recording was made when Katy was just twenty, and the track 'Broken' had been intended to be the single from the album, although it was never released. It's a mark of how far preparations for the album had gone

that there was even a video to accompany 'Broken', with Katy sharing the microphone with Adam, looking more than ever like something out of the 1950s. In later years Katy revealed that she'd been encouraged to emulate Avril Lavigne at the time, and one critic reported that the track sounded like 'an April Lavigne cast-off'.

The Matrix denied that they were cashing in on Katy's soaring popularity. 'We don't want to be pop stars and we're not releasing it on a major label,' said Lauren Christy. 'And it's not called Katy Perry and The Matrix. These are just great songs and I'm very proud of it.' That was certainly true: the album was only briefly available and can now just be bought online second-hand.

Katy and Adam duetted on seven of the album's ten songs, with Katy going solo on three, and a further three tracks were recorded, though they don't appear on the album. This wasn't the only blast from the past for Katy. A year earlier the teen idol Miley Cyrus had had a massive hit with the song 'Breakout', written by Ted Bruner, Trey Vittetoe and Gina Schock of the Go-Go's, and as Katy's star shone ever brighter, the news emerged that she had originally recorded it for her album *One of the Boys*. In the end it hadn't gone on the album, but had been passed on to Miley instead. Miley had liked it so much she made it the title track of the album: it was 'one of [her] favorite songs as moms, dads, sisters, brothers can, you know, relate to it. And it's basically because you just want to go out and have fun with your friends and sometimes, you know, go out dancing and let loose once in a while'.

So far, so normal in the pop world, but there was an extra dimension that was not. Miley wasn't just given the song: she was also given the recorded backing vocals, which were sung by none other than Katy. 'My vocals are actually on "Breakout",' Katy told *Bliss* magazine. 'I thought, "Yes, I'm singing on a Miley single."' It all helped contribute to the prevailing impression that Katy was everywhere.

In the meantime Katy was being signed up for some big-name festivals across the globe, such as the San Remo Song Festival in Italy, and all the while she continued to tease her audiences about her singleton status. 'So I didn't find a man in Denmark, I didn't find a man in Manchester, anyone here want to come home with me?' she asked a London audience. The crowd cheered.

The reviews continued to be positive: 'Perry has the personality and the experience of how to work a crowd that will ensure she's more than just the next Avril Lavigne,' said the *Independent*. 'She's at her best on songs such as "Ur So Gay", which in spite of its questionable lyrics is a brilliant attack on a former lover – during it she urges all the girls to phone their exes so they can listen.' Katy's rapport with the audience was becoming ever more self-assured.

Not everyone was a fan, however. In an astonishing broadside, the singer Lulu, who achieved success in the considerably more innocent climate of the 1960s, lashed out at the overt sexualization of today's young female stars, and Katy's was one of the names she picked on,

alongside the Pussycat Dolls and Girls Aloud. All of them came in for a tongue-lashing.

'It's cheapened the music and it is exploitative,' she told the *Daily Record*, complaining of the raunchy nature of today's music business. 'I would never have stripped off like that and gyrated up and down a pole. There are talented kids who don't need to do that but it is just expected of them. It's so regressive. I feel bad for them. To be a singer, you have to be naked and do things with your body and men on video. What has that got to do with the music? I would not want to be launching a career now. Nowadays you have to achieve world domination or you get dropped by the record company. If the first single's not a hit, you're out. Today, to be successful, it is not enough to be a good singer. You have to have an army of people all focusing on that goal relentlessly. You don't just have to have talent and appeal – there has to be a big strategy. You have to be able to hold your head together, because the celebrity thing is out of whack. I think it's crazy.'

That was as maybe, but Katy was still managing to triumph in this admittedly difficult world. She didn't take anything for granted, though. Having spent such a long time waiting for her breakthrough, she was all too aware that it could disappear again just like that. 'There are about 500 other girls who are desperate to be in my position, I can't take anything for granted,' she told the *Daily Record*, although she probably underestimated the number of hopefuls waiting to claw their way up the ladder. Many years

earlier, Katy's idol Madonna stepped into a slot temporarily vacated by Debbie Harry when her partner became ill. The vacation turned out to be anything but temporary and Madonna walked into the stratosphere while, for many years, Debbie lost her way. It's a salutary story for any rising star.

'I remember living in Beverly Hills and having a new black car, being very comfortable on my monthly wage, and my cousin looked at me and said, "Katy, this can go away," and I was like, "It's never going to go away." And then it did. I recall that moment so clearly when I would write a cheque for my rent with $15 in my bank account and on the memo I would write, "God, please help." So this is an important time in my life. During the next two or three years, if I do things right, I will have a real career, and if I don't I'll just be that girl who kissed a girl.'

It was a far more pragmatic approach than that taken by many of her contemporaries, and it was born directly out of her early experiences. It was becoming more and more apparent that although it hadn't felt that way at the time, those early years had done her a power of good. When you have to work hard for success, you realize you'll have to work even harder to maintain it, and with the incessant touring she was doing, crossing and re-crossing the globe, Katy was showing she had what it takes. And the initial signs were good: on 9 February 2009, 'I Kissed A Girl' and 'Hot N Cold' were both certified three times platinum by the Recording Industry Association of America for individual digital sales of over three million. While her career hit new heights, Katy talked down the idea of marriage

and children, saying that she would have to wait until she was in her thirties, but in actual fact, the coup de foudre that would throw her and Russell together was only a few short months away.

On the press front, although Katy had bowed out of it, the feud between Perez and Lily Allen was still going strong: the latest round started when Perez suggested he should have a role in her new video.

Lily wasn't slow off the mark: 'Oh, I'm sorry, we've already cast the jealous and bitter lonely old queen role. Next time eh?' she tweeted.

Perez: 'Jealous of who? David Beckham, maybe. And if I wanted to be a fucked-up Brit, I'd rather be Amy Winehouse – whose [sic] got talent.'

Lily: 'You're like so obsessed with me it's embarassing [sic].'

Perez: 'Congrats on your album doing well in America, though. It's REALLY HARD to sell copies when u discount it to $3.99. Desperate!'

Lily: 'It's also number one everywhere else in the world douchebag. Go away you little parasite.'

Perez: 'Aw, u can see I've lost weight! I am a littler Perez. But I'm still a big fat cunt – just like U! That's why I lova ya. xoxo.' And so it went on, ad nauseum. It was still part of the Katy story, though, because she and Perez were closer than ever, to say nothing of the fact that Katy was now part of the mainstream showbusiness world that spends its entire time gossiping about itself. Meanwhile, the gossip about Katy's love life continued: she was back

with Travis for the moment, but that wasn't going to last for long.

Katy's sense of style had been much commented on since she'd stepped into the limelight, and one of the benefits of her success was that she got to indulge her love of clothes. It was something that gave a number of young designers a unique opportunity if they played their cards right.

'One girl contacted me on MySpace wanting to design for me,' Katy told the *Observer*. 'I wear her costumes because they're so darn cute, like her pink romper with red glittering lips on the front of it. It doesn't matter what you wear on stage, so long as you sound good, but I love to go that extra jump. Lady Gaga has the coolest outfits. I was texting her the other day, asking where she gets her clothes. At home I sit around in a zebra-print romper suit from H&M. Rompers are very me. They're super-easy to run around in. With anything you wear, it's about having confidence. A lot of people see me and think: she pulls off so many things that a lot of people can't pull off. It's fantastic to show off your personality through what you're wearing. You can give off an energy or a vibe just by wearing a silly, cute, light-hearted, smack-a-smile-on-your-face style. Why not? I'm young. I like to have fun. I don't come off as boring.' The mention of H&M was no coincidence either as Katy had signed up for the company's Fashion Against Aids campaign.

Texting Lady Gaga! This was real success. The two women had more in common than it would initially appear,

for although Lady Gaga had come from a burlesque background and achieved success considerably more quickly than Katy, both were the real deal. They both had talent and, crucially, neither of them was the manufactured product of a reality TV show. Both women were opinionated and in charge of their careers, and they were both very striking, although in quite different ways. Lady Gaga, with her constantly changing appearance and outrageous outfits, was more art house, while Katy was more mainstream, but they were fully aware of the importance of their looks. They were also very, very ambitious, so perhaps it's not surprising that they found lots to text about.

Katy was being asked about her sense of style a lot these days. While she wore plenty of contemporary designers, she had the retro vibe off to a T, and there was a great deal of curiosity about where she got her clothes. Just Jared, a website that covers all things celebrity, asked her where she shopped when she was in New York. 'There are a couple places, I go to the Lower East Side because I like more of the little boutiquey stuff,' Katy replied. 'I love this one shop called Mandate of Heaven. She is my favorite, she does rompers and jumpers. I just bought this pink jumper. It has a portrait of a kitten on it and it's really short so it shows off my butt a little. But it's very innocent, very Lolita. So if you come to NYC you have to check out Mandate of Heaven!' For the boutique, it was the kind of publicity that money just couldn't buy. Everywhere you looked, people copied Katy's look, shopped where she shopped and followed her every move with slavish attention. And

even if the attention had started to fade at this stage, Katy would still have made her mark on pop history. As it was, though, she'd hardly got started – and the best was very much still to come.

Gambling on Success

Katy continued to be very much in demand, flitting back and forth across the Atlantic, one moment in the UK on *Later . . . With Jools Holland* and *Ant and Dec's Saturday Night Takeaway*; the next appearing in the US on *American Idol*, in which she sported a female version of Elvis Presley's famous white jumpsuit to sing her next single, 'Waking Up In Vegas' – and with her black hair and red lips, there was a genuine resemblance, too.

'Waking Up In Vegas' was the fourth and final single from her album *One of the Boys*. Written by Katy, Desmond Child and Andreas Carlsson, produced by Greg Wells and co-produced by Katy, one publicity shot had Katy posing in a little pink minidress alongside two giant red dice. Released in April 2009, it got to a respectable No 9 whilst staying in the Top 15 for three months, and told the story of an off-the-cuff road trip to the famous American town. 'Vegas gives me that "what the fuck feeling",' Katy told the *Sun*. 'It's really close to LA, so one night you could be having a beer with your friends and, when you wake up, you're in Vegas.'

In fact, it hinted at one of the wilder moments in Katy's life, a spur-of-the-moment Vegas wedding, although unlike

so many stars who do it for real and live to regret it, Katy's was all pretend.

'I was 21,' Katy told PopEater about an escapade with an ex-boyfriend. 'We took all the pictures with the minister, with the fake cake, in the fake chapel and got a fake marriage certificate. We went and bought a wedding dress and a suit at a thrift store, and scanned the pictures and the certificate to my family members, my manager at the time [and] totally freaked the shit out of them. It was the most hilarious, stupid prank I've ever pulled, I still have the wedding dress and the certificate.'

The single made up for the relative disappointment of her third single, 'Thinking Of You', and its success proved that Katy was well enough established to have the odd duff number, which wasn't something she could have done when she was just starting out. By the time she came to work with them, Andreas Carlsson and Desmond Child were an established team. Andreas gave an interview to Hit-Quarters, in which he described how the song came to be put together. 'Katy was instantly recognized by Desmond and me as somebody who has the talent of Madonna,' he began. 'I've said it many times – I think she is the most talented artist that I've ever come across, and I think she has a huge career in front of her. We really wanted to tell the story that described that moment when everybody's checking out on Vegas after they've had their fun. And Katy is the perfect artist to tell such a story – she has humour, and she knows how to deliver it. I already had the guitar riff of the song. The phrase "put your money where

your mouth is" was something that we always wanted to use – it was almost the title, but ended up in the chorus. I don't know where that Vegas thing came from, but I was a big Elvis fan and it just seemed right at the time.'

On the whole the critics were positive. Billboard called it Katy's 'most radio-friendly song yet'. 'If you were told that Katy Perry was releasing a single called "Waking Up In Vegas", what would you expect?' wrote Nick Levine on Digital Spy. 'A cheeky tale of drunken debauchery and a video featuring loads of poker, Perry in a showgirl outfit and . . . erm . . . an actual elephant? Yup, that's pretty much exactly what she's given us. But even though Vegas feels a little obvious, it's still hard not to get sucked in. Opening with the sound of slot machines, this is a giddy pop-rock romp featuring an ace sing-along chorus . . . Proof that when she's not trying too hard to be outrageous, Perry can be lots of fun.'

'This is the sound of some of the top talents in the pop music industry working together,' reported About.com. 'Producer Greg Wells has hit paydirt recently with Mika's "Grace Kelly" and Timbaland and OneRepublic's "Apologize". Desmond Child is a veteran in the Songwriter's Hall of Fame and Andreas Carlsson first gained notice as an associate of Max Martin. All of this talent combined does not disappoint here.'

The video was as lively as you would expect and was directed by Joseph Kahn, who had done a great deal with Britney Spears in the past, so knew Katy's target market inside out. He had directed Britney in the videos for 'Womanizer', 'Stronger' and 'Toxic', and he'd also directed

Eminem in 'We Made You' and 'Without Me', which won him a Grammy and VMA in 2002.

Filmed in Las Vegas in March 2009, the routine kicks off with Katy holding hands with her boyfriend, played by Joel David Moore, in a laundromat in front of a slot machine. Joel puts a coin into the slot, and when three "blazing 7" symbols come up the couple are showered in quarters. They go on to win at roulette, run to their hotel room, where they kick out Vegas magic act Penn & Teller, then win millions more by defeating the poker pro Daniel Negreanu. After that they're welcomed into the Palms Hotel by Gavin and George J. Maloof, who own it, race each other through Vegas in his and hers Lamborghinis and finally end up dressed for a Las Vegas show, riding chariots down Fremont Street, with a fire-eater and an elephant, before taking part in a Roman feast surrounded by Elvis impersonators.

The couple then kiss in a money booth, after which their luck totally changes. They argue, lose everything, are thrown out of their hotel room, which Penn & Teller grab back while performing a card trick, and Katy is forced to steal food from a room-service tray before they end up back in the laundromat. Joel puts a coin in the slot, three "blazing 7" symbols come up, the quarters begin to spin out . . . and the video fades.

The video was a lot of fun, very poppy and jolly, and it turned out to be something of a family affair, too. 'If you look at the opening scene, which is kind of the way we ended as well, you will see a little old lady to the left with

like an oxygen tank on [folding laundry],' Katy told Just Jared. 'If you are on the outskirts of Vegas, it can get really depressing. You'll see old people with their gambling carts and you'll be like, "Ew, you need the Lord!" That little old lady is my 88-year-old grandma! She lives in Las Vegas and she was dying to be in the video.' And she was, with her effervescent granddaughter in front of her.

Katy was beginning to show that she could pull in some seriously big names, too. Joel David Moore, who appeared alongside her, was an up-and-coming talent, having appeared in *Six Feet Under*, *House* and *Bones*, as well as *Dodgeball* and *Avatar*. He'd also appeared in a number of advertisements, so was very familiar to American audiences.

The location throughout was the Palms Resort, which, coincidentally, was where Gym Class Heroes' 'Clothes Off' video was made, as well as Eminem's 'We Made You', and high-profile glitzy designer Bob Mackie – creator of Cher's black feathered dress at the 1986 Oscars – supplied the costumes from his personal collection. The video was a smash hit, with over 20 million YouTube views.

Katy was on a roll, even though she had once again split up with Travis, thus renewing interest in her personal life. Having been invited to perform at Vienna's Life Ball, one of the biggest charity events in Europe, she flitted across the Atlantic and made a spectacular entrance onto a stunning marine-themed set. Perched in a giant oyster shell, she was lowered onto a stage that appeared to be deep under the sea wearing a tight-fitting leotard bedecked with shells. Other high-profile guests included Bill Clinton,

Pamela Anderson and Eva Longoria Parker, while her fellow performer was Roisin Murphy.

It was quite a night. Held to raise money to fight HIV/AIDS, 2.5 million litres of water were trucked in to surround the town hall and 40,000 people attended, many of whom were wearing outrageous outfits, bedecked with anchor-shaped nipple clamps, starfish, body paint, mermaids and mermen. 'My only complaint is that every time someone asks for a picture with me I walk away covered in body glitter,' said a good-natured Katy. 'But I've been covered in worse.'

However, there were downsides to Katy's fame, too. After her spat with Lily Allen, she now found herself caught up in an even bigger controversy with a clothes designer called Katie Perry, who ran an eponymous fashion label in Australia. There were reports that Katy wasn't happy about this, and matters came to a head when Katie lodged a trademark application for her business name, something that resulted in a legal exchange with Katy's law firm, Fisher Adams Kelly.

'On 9 June, I went to pick up some mail and received a 30-page letter from Fisher Adams Kelly, who represent Katheryn Hudson, opposing the use of my trademark and asking me to pull my trademark, stop using advertising and sign the attached letter or face legal proceedings,' Katie related to website Smart Company. 'My next course of action is that I'm going to make sure I'm at that hearing on 10 July to explain why they shouldn't get an extension of time. I started my label before she was known here. I've

worked hard building up my brand, everything is made in Australia, I'm building up a great reputation, and to have someone receive those statements from lawyers saying I can't do that is distressing. It's also intimidating, I've never had to deal with lawyers and legal things like this before. They actually contacted me this morning, and said they are going back to their clients. They are realising I'm not a pirate trying to make money from the singer Katy Perry, which if they checked my website they should have found that out.'

It appears that Katy's lawyers hadn't realized that Katie Perry had been operating under her own name for years, and the case was subsequently dropped, with no further action being taken. Nor was there any evidence that Katy had been involved in the case. However, it illustrates the fact that a lot of money was at stake now, and that Katy needed to be protected. She wasn't just a successful singer: she was big business and millions were at stake.

However, the whole issue had been very distressing for Katie, who'd had to shell out AUS $12,000 in legal fees. 'I just resigned myself to seven years of being in a mess, but I wasn't going to give up,' she told My Small Business. 'It was very personal, and using my own name felt like a personal attack. I feel lucky, and also that I came to lawyers, and that I had good representation.' Nevertheless, it had been an unpleasant experience for both sides.

Katy didn't have time to brood, though. If she wanted to last the distance, she was going to have to keep reinventing herself, as Madonna has done so successfully.

Consequently, she kept experimenting with new ways to present herself, including appearing in raunchy black leather for a photoshoot with *Complex* magazine.

'It is a bit of a darker side for me,' she said in the accompanying interview. 'It was a little S&M and I liked it! But I did have to hang from a cage, which could have easily gone wrong with the five-inch heels I was wearing. I do it [dressing up] every single night, full-blown drag-queen style – hair, make-up, everything. There'll be a costume, there'll be some hot pants, there'll be some legs. God gave me these boobs and I use them to my greatest extent. I'm not Jennifer Lopez but the hourglass is there. People are always like, "Well, yours are fake," and I'm like, "No, I just don't go around screaming they're not fake." It's all about doing push-ups. The push-ups keep them good and not like armpit pancakes.'

Katy's relentless globetrotting continued as she headed East to the MTV Japan Awards, but so did the continual carping. Lily Allen was about to start up again, but before she did, the lesbian singer Beth Ditto launched an attack, on the now familiar grounds that Katy was playing with lesbian chic. 'I Kissed A Girl' was a 'dyke anthem for straight girls who like to turn guys on by making out they are gay or like faking gay', she snapped in an interview in *Attitude* magazine. 'I hate Katy Perry! She's offensive to gay culture, I'm so offended. She's just riding on the backs of our culture, without having to pay any of the dues and not being actually lesbian or anything at all. She's on the cover of a fucking gay magazine.'

Once again, Katy rose above it, showing every sign of enjoying her notoriety. Up on stage, she not only engaged with the audience, she came across as a slightly older naughty sister. There was never anything threatening about her — even in her most revealing dresses and most provocative poses, Katy was still essentially a nice girl who didn't smoke, do drugs, drink excessively or sleep around; instead she came across as the kind of girl who would stay up too late and hold midnight feasts in the dorm. 'I feel very influential at this crucial moment in your life,' she would tell her audiences, before inciting them to use a naughty word in front of their parents: penis. It was pretty harmless stuff, but it amused the crowd, kept everyone's spirits up and gave her just a frisson of rebellion.

She continued to garner industry respect, too, with Queen's Brian May making a point of praising her, saying, 'She's gorgeous.' Men absolutely loved her, which is one reason the 'real' lesbian crowd weren't so happy about what they felt she represented, and she seemed to have as many adult male fans as she did teenybopper female ones. Men appreciated Katy on a different level, too. To them, she was naughty but nice; the girl who looks like a bad girl but acts like a good girl; the prom princess in grown-up form.

It didn't hurt that in real life, she preferred boys to girls, either. 'I'm into guys, that's clear from my relationship with Travis,' she told the *Mirror*. 'I'm a lot better behaved than some people would think. I've never been one to jump between relationships and sleep around. I'm not casual at all. I've always been into making a connection with someone.

That's what it's all about for me. Besides, it's sexier to be mysterious and not give it away. I never hook up . . . If I really like a person then I'll go on a date. But you'll never catch me just randomly making out with someone.'

As such, she was a far better role model than many people realized. Katy did *love*, not *sex*, whatever her audiences might think. That sense of utter security in herself, which translated into total self-confidence, was a product of her childhood that was now coming into its own. Sheltered she might have been, but her parents had done a fantastically good job of preparing her for life out in the world. It's a paradox that a childhood within a very strict community seemed to have prepared her for life in one of the most potentially exploitative industries in the world.

Katy certainly needed her self-confidence, as despite all the support she was getting – and an increasing number of men were only too happy to voice their attraction to her – she had to put up with a huge amount of sniping. It was noticeable that a lot of this came from other women. Not content to let matters rest, Lily Allen soon took up cudgels again: 'It's very odd isn't it [about her image],' she told the *Daily Record*. 'I don't really like her. I think it's all quite contrived. I know what it is and it doesn't come from her, it's not written by her, it's written by other people. So I think it's quite sinister to be like "we need to create a character . . . and a story". It just doesn't mean anything to me. It's just marketing, isn't it? I'm sure that she's quite a sweet person, but I just don't really agree with the whole thing.' And as for that threat to put Katy's number on Facebook:

'That's not slagging her off,' Lily continued. 'I just said I was a bit frosty with her, because she'd slagged me. Slagging off is saying "you're shit". She compared herself to me and Amy Winehouse and I just politely said that's quite an interesting comparison to make – you're not English, and you don't write your own songs. It's not slagging someone off, it's just stating the obvious.' It also sounded a little like jealousy. There was no denying that Katy was the hottest new thing around and that she'd be bigger, perhaps, than Lily or Amy. Certainly her male fan base was growing by the day.

Katy's popularity was definitely not in doubt. During the festival season in the summer of 2009, no gig was complete without Katy: she got a massive welcome at T in the Park in Scotland, where she appeared on stage with a giant strawberry and deployed her customary charm to one interviewer. 'I'm loving it here but I kind of can't believe that I'm here, hanging out with all the cool rock guys,' she said. 'It's like the nerdy kid from school accidentally ending up getting invited to the cool kids' party. But it's great, though. Here in Europe, you guys do festivals better than anyone else in the world. It's a real rite of passage thing – it hasn't gone that far in the States. It is getting there, we are trying but we don't have the same sense of culture around it all that you guys do. I love festivals here.' That was really laying it on: for an American to come to Britain and talk about the fact that it was better in the UK was bound to win round the few doubters left.

Katy's showmanship was very much in evidence during

the gig when she appeared as the track 'California Gurls' played in the background. A pink flag with Katy's name on it was draped across the stage and there was an abundance of plastic flamingoes and strawberries, which were later thrown into the crowd. Katy's costumes were becoming increasingly flamboyant, too, with sequined ladybird corset tops, mini shorts and lots of bows on display. Tutus and polka dots also featured highly, and at times Katy almost seemed to be making fun of herself.

There were also signs of weariness, but Katy realized that this was her time and she wasn't going to blow it, so she continued to cross the world, paying a short trip to Australia before returning to the UK. On arrival in Glasgow, Katy shocked onlookers by having a massive temper tantrum as she went through airport security. Staff insisted on checking her five suitcases, and after the long and exhausting trip, Katy blew her top.

It was very uncharacteristic behaviour, but Katy was totally unrepentant afterwards. 'I swear, I never feel more like cattle than when I have to go through airport security,' she said. 'They hate their lives and they hate us for sure. By the last flight, the third time going through security, I lost it on a security person.' It was stress and tiredness, of course, and it was taking its toll.

Katy herself recognized that this was the price she had to pay. 'I always seem to be out on the road but it's a great thing because I feel that people have got to see that it's not manufactured – I'm out there in the trenches,' she told the *Daily Star*. 'I've been working for a year and a half straight.

I start writing for the next album in October so I'm going to go away for a minute and order some room service and get a tan somewhere.' Not that there was really much time for that.

A collaboration with dance supremo Calvin Harris was on the cards, although doubts were being cast over whether the work could be done on the grounds that Calvin had become too famous in his own right. Katy was very keen for it to happen, though. 'I'm more excited about European music than anything America brings out – you guys always have the cooler edge,' she told the *Daily Star*. 'Events like festivals are so important here. We don't have that in the States. I'm so excited about working with Calvin – I've noticed I'm missing making the people move a little bit. As he's so good at making the crowd move, I could use a little of what he's cooking up. I want some of The Cardigans meet Ace of Base. I'm a huge fan of pop songs which never get old but I'm not going to throw a bunch of people on the record just so it sells.'

As the summer progressed, it was announced that Katy would appear at the MTV Awards – it was to prove a momentous evening as someone else seemed to be on her mind. In hindsight, it's easy to read too much into a throw-away remark, but Katy appeared not to have forgotten a certain man she was briefly acquainted with. In an interview, right out of the blue, she brought up the subject of Russell Brand. 'I had heard all about his reputation and I have to agree he has a certain *je ne sais quoi*,' she told the *Daily Express*. Meanwhile, Russell had been talking about

how charming Katy was. The fates appeared to be mar-shalling their next meeting in the wings.

Such throwaway remarks hadn't been noticed by the press as yet, though, and most of the gossip surrounding Katy involved Calvin Harris, with whom Katy was spotted dining in Glasgow, although the only thing on the agenda that night was work. In the meantime, Russell tweeted ecstatically when he discovered that he and Katy would be staying in the same hotel in New York: 'Nude on my bal-cony,' he wrote. 'I imagine they'll send Spitfires to shoot me down like King Kong – due to my gorilla privates, not because I'm hairy. Katy Perry is moving into the hotel room opposite. I'm stealing a room service uniform. A female one, obviously – cherry chapstick delivery. Right, I've got to deliver some kinky breakfast. Wish me luck.'

In fact, the two of them were in New York for the same reason: the MTV VMAs. Having been forgiven for the previous year's performance, Russell had been invited to host the ceremony. Judging from his tweets, he was getting very overexcited about the night ahead. 'I am doing a big entrance with Katy Perry. I can confirm Katy is involved in my entrance, and I'm hoping I'll be . . . you can finish the rest!' he proclaimed. 'It's really exciting cos I now know what to expect and just to enjoy it. It's interesting to be part of the centre of pop culture for a couple of hours. To see my name outside Radio City Hall – well, that's amaz-ing. I didn't expect that so it was really nice.' In actual fact, Russell's life was going to change even more than he could have dreamt that night. Katy didn't win an award, but there

was a hint of what was to come when Russell publicly commented, 'Katy Perry didn't win an award and she's staying at the same hotel as me, so she's gonna need a shoulder to cry on. So in a way, I'm the real winner tonight.' It wasn't quite that fast, but it didn't take long. In fact, she more than stood up to him. 'I was 25, 30 feet away from him [when he said that]. And I threw the bottle straight at him. Hit him smack dab on the head,' she told *Esquire*. 'Can you imagine the horrible feeling he had when he was used to getting everything he wanted? I was like, "You've met your match."'

In the event, the first reports of the VMAs centred not on what would quickly become a passionate and high-profile romance, but on the behaviour of Kanye West. When Taylor Swift was given the Best Female Video award Kanye made an idiot of himself by going on stage during her speech and announcing that the award should have gone to Beyoncé. Meanwhile, Beyoncé sat in the audience, looking mortified. People queued up to denounce him and Katy, a friend of Taylor's, was one of the first. 'Fuck you, Kanye,' she spat. 'It was like you stepped on a kitten.' Kanye issued a blustering apology but everyone was disgusted. Later reports centred on the after-show party, where Russell and Katy had been inseparable, it emerged. 'They were flirting and whispering all night,' said one observer. 'Russell looked extremely pleased with himself.'

As well he might do. Russell sent Katy a poem and asked for one in return. She replied by sending him a picture of her cleavage with the word 'Poem' written on it. Russell

was beside himself; he 'killed himself laughing', according to reports at the time. Both knew they were smitten, and although Katy later said that she made Russell wait for sex (for a whole week), it wasn't long before they were spotted on a romantic break in Thailand together. That alone should have alerted the world that something was up. Katy had been working so hard that up until now a holiday would have been out of the question, but now that she'd met Russell, it seemed that something else was on her mind apart from her music career.

As the news of their romance spread, no one could quite believe it. Squeaky-clean little Katy with an ex-junkie, ex-alcoholic sex addict? In actual fact, this is a little unfair, given that Russell had given up two of those vices by this time. But even so . . .

Perez Hilton hit his blog: 'We're not gonna lie, this new couple is kinda hot bizarre!

'Supposedly after hitting it off at the VMAs, British Lothario Russell Brand whisked Katy Perry away to Thailand for a week-long lovers' vacay!

'Though Katy didn't mention Brand specifically, she Twittered about her trip: "After a week in magical Thailand I'm ready to face the real world again. Been schooled on Morrissey, Oscar Wilde & Peter Sellers . . . inspired."

'Russell Brand is known for his admiration of the three men, hinting at their new romance.

'The twosome supposedly shared a kiss at Lady Gaga's VMA after-party and since then they haven't stopped the flirtation.

'We're very interested to see how this relationship develops!'

Perez and everyone else. Global curiosity was stoked further when Katy tweeted, 'Pssst . . . I've got a secret. HUGE news coming in a couple days. No, my ego is not prego.' The couple were spotted back in the UK together, visiting the house of Jonathan Ross, with whom Russell had kept in touch. The two then left for Paris Fashion Week, where they were spotted out at parties together, although Russell couldn't help himself, tweeting, 'I'm in "Gay Paris" – I swear by the time I leave it'll be known as "Hetero Paris". Or at least "Bi Paris".' It was typical Russell, but was it all aimed at Katy? The incredulous public was beginning to realize this was serious and not just a fling.

That the pair were attracted to each other – wildly so, in fact – was not in doubt, but Katy was also exactly the sort of person Russell needed. She stood up to him, did not allow herself to be treated as a conquest and had a status equal to his. For all that Russell had delighted in his Lothario image, meeting a woman who didn't capitulate to him on the first date and gave as good as she got was a revelation. For the first time in his entire life, Russell was falling in love.

He was only too happy to admit to it, too. 'I think I'm in love,' he said, as Britain's female population prepared to shed a tear.

Across the Atlantic, however, another couple were keeping a very close eye on the developing relationship:

Katy's parents, Keith and Mary. They hadn't commented on the situation yet, but one of their congregation, who prefers not to be named, saw it all at close hand. 'Keith and Mary were praying that this wasn't just a shallow Hollywood fling, and by all accounts it wasn't,' he said. 'They're so protective of their daughter and I think deep down they wished she'd remained a Christian singer rather than going into mainstream pop.'

Interestingly, however, even back then, well before it was obvious how serious the relationship was going to become, Keith and Mary made it clear that they hoped the pair would wed. And that, perhaps, is the clue as to why Russell wanted Katy when he'd had everyone else: because she was a nice girl whose parents expected her boyfriend to behave properly, or, to put it another way, she expected to be treated with respect. With the best will in the world, the same could not be said of many of Russell's former girlfriends. In Katy, it seemed he'd found a class act.

Rusty Braunstein

From the moment Katy and Russell got together, they were inseparable, and while they might have seemed an unlikely couple to the rest of the world, it clearly didn't bother either of them in the slightest. For whatever reason, Katy was right for Russell and Russell was right for Katy, and their relationship proved to be very serious indeed. What the doubters tended to forget about Russell was that while he was extremely wild at one stage, his drink and drugs years were behind him and his sex addiction was about to go the same way. To have as many partners as Russell went beyond the ordinary appetites of a young man, making it clear that he had replaced his former addictions with sex. But now, for the first time in his life, he appeared to have found real love.

Russell wanted to give up his old life. Huge amounts of sex with vast numbers of partners might seem like a dream to most young men, but in reality it's a pretty empty lifestyle, and he was beginning to tire of it. Russell met Katy at exactly the right moment: he was ready to settle down. 'I am living in a different way at the moment, regardless of what happens in my current situation,' Russell told *The Sunday Times*. 'I am unlikely to be satisfied with the calamitous promiscuity of the preceding five or six years.'

The change in Katy's lifestyle was not so dramatic. She had always been a serial monogamist, having only had a handful of boyfriends, all of whom had been serious. She had even come close to getting engaged to Travis, because, quite simply, she was that kind of a girl. It's also telling that after the wildness of his youth, Russell chose a nice Christian girl to settle down with; Katy, meanwhile, was well aware of the contradiction between the sexy way she presented herself and who she really was.

Travis, unsurprisingly, was gutted by the turn of events and lashed out by predicting that the relationship would fail. Who could blame him? Katy was beautiful, young, successful and a major catch; the two had seemed destined to be together but now the relationship had failed. To add to the hurt, Katy hadn't so much moved on as stepped into a whole new life, for Russell was also quite a catch: you don't attract that many women without having something to say for yourself. Travis was forced to watch miserably from the sidelines, telling friends that Katy was fundamentally a goody two shoes and that Russell would soon get bored. He was right about the first half of that statement, and wrong about the second: it seemed Russell wanted a goody two shoes, which made Katy exactly right for him. Russell's exes weren't much happier about the situation: Georgina Baillie (she of the Sachs-gate tapes) allowed herself a catty remark: 'You don't date Russell seriously,' she said. 'He likes the idea of a serious relationship but when you've got all these different flavours of ice

cream offered to you on a plate, you're not going to stick with vanilla, are you?' She, too, would be proved wrong.

Not that Katy presented herself as vanilla, as she demonstrated by being photographed wearing stockings and suspenders – she was one of a breed of celebrities credited with boosting exotic lingerie sales – while the couple's passion became more and more public. They were constantly photographed throwing themselves at one another: 'Get a room,' begged the papers as it became increasingly clear that this was far more than just a fling.

Katy turned twenty-five and celebrated it with a party at the Sunset Beach in LA to which everyone was ordered to wear white. Russell, of course, was present, as were Perez Hilton and Katy's friend Taylor Swift. The theme was Willy Wonka and the Chocolate Factory, with Oompa Loompas everywhere. After a formal(ish) sit-down dinner, there was a huge paint fight at the end and everyone got spattered. It was all very Katy: silly, good-humoured and an awful lot of fun.

The bond between Russell and Katy was obvious to everyone present. At one point Russell got down on his knees and presented Katy with a huge lollipop, which she took and pretended to knight him with. Although they joined in the fun with the rest of the guests, they could hardly tear themselves away from each other, making it absolutely clear how important the relationship was to both of them. They had, at this stage, only been together for about a month, but they still gave the impression of

being a long-term couple. The doubters had clearly been utterly wrong.

Both Katy and Russell had extremely busy schedules, and now things became even more hectic because, although neither of them had much free time, they were determined to spend it together. As a result they began jetting to far-flung cities around the world for brief rendezvous, enabling their relationship to flourish – at least the two of them could afford the convenience of private jets! And in the way that couples who have just got together do, neither could stop talking about the other. Given that they were both extremely famous, that inevitably involved talking about their relationship to the press. At the Music Industry Trust Awards, the *Mirror* managed to have a word with Russell: 'You have made me blush, but to be honest I haven't stopped smiling,' he cooed. 'She's a lovely girl and it's going really, really well. In fact I've never felt more settled in all of my life. Katy is fantastic. I'm really happy.'

Russell's friends, who were more accustomed to him being a manic bed-hopper, could hardly believe their eyes. 'We've never seen him like this,' one said at the time, adding presciently. 'He always has a woman on his arm, or in his bed, and hasn't been interested in monogamy. But this is different – we all think it won't be long before he marries Katy. She's a little bit crazy and freewilled like Russell and the pair of them seem to have met their match. They have a good laugh together. I'm waiting for a call to say they are in that Little Chapel in Vegas and have run off to get

married.' In the event it wouldn't happen quite like that, but it was a perceptive remark, nonetheless.

Russell fuelled speculation, too. He seemed to find it frustrating that people didn't realize he'd grown up and wasn't the wild-living creature of yesteryear. Asked if he was feeling broody, he replied, 'I am, actually. It's seven years since I took drugs. I've made a film. I don't think I have to fight so much – I've grown weary of the carousel.' But still amazement about the unlikely duo lingered.

With so much attention focused on Katy's personal life, it was sometimes difficult to remember she had a professional one, too. Her career was progressing as strongly as ever, with constant touring, an appearance on *MTV Unplugged* and a live album based on the performance including two new tracks, 'Brick By Brick' and 'Hackensack', which was released in November 2009. There were also appearances on the singles of two other artists, a remix of 3OH!3's 'Starstrukk' and Timbaland's 'If We Ever Meet Again'. It was quite a schedule, even without the distraction of a new romance, but there were benefits. Katy and Russell were learning what so many other famous celebrity couples have discovered – Brad and Angelina spring to mind – that while separately they were big news, together they were a sensation. Both had a big enough profile before, but now scarcely a day went by without them being mentioned in the press.

Katy's private life was crossing over into her public life, too, as Russell began having an effect on her costumes, as well as everything else. She told the *Mirror* that revealing

clothes were high on the list: 'I've gone for less costume changes this year but less clothing too,' she said. 'It's all a bit naughtier, with lace, crystals, feathers, bowler hats and a lot of boobie things. I've gone for a dark, romantic vibe. It's sexy. I'm sexy. I'm highlighting what God gave me — what mama made. I will be especially naughty under Russell's influence. I've worn things in the past couple of months that aren't appropriate for this press conference because of him. Sorry Mother, sorry Father.'

There was a good deal of competition on the music scene, from the likes of Lady Gaga and Beyoncé to name but two, but Katy had no problem continuing to make headlines wherever she went. She was as good-looking as Beyoncé and not quite as odd as Lady Gaga but as talented as both of them, while her romance with Russell continued to add a level of intrigue. Katy hosted November's MTV European Music Awards in Berlin, and while Beyoncé won almost every award going, it was Katy who attracted the most attention just by being there. Then, as if to make a point, Katy performed cover versions of 'Poker Face' and 'Single Ladies': 'I'm totally petrified about what those girls will think, but I'm doing it in my own way, not to be taken too seriously — like everything I do,' she said. In the event, she hid her fears well.

Russell, meanwhile, was as loved-up as ever. 'I've taken a pledge. I can't break it now. There will be no more three-somes,' he declared. There were even rumours that the happy couple were looking for a place in LA to move into together. Russell applied for a passport for his cat and

even put his Hampstead home up for sale, although he denied that he was moving to the States. No one could quite believe that such a notorious womanizer had finally been tamed, despite the signs to the contrary. Katy even had a nickname for him: Rusty Braunstein (Rusty had long been Russell's nickname elsewhere).

As far as Russell was concerned, life really couldn't have been any better. Just a couple of years earlier, after the Sachs-gate debacle, his life had seemed in a mess; now he was upsetting people again by suggesting that the scandal surrounding the phone call had been the making of him. Far from being repentant, Russell even went so far as to blame Andrew for not picking up the phone. (In fairness, Andrew Sachs also pointed out that it had put his own name back in the limelight for the first time in years.)

'I am really happy with what I am doing now – happy in my personal life and happy with my professional life,' he told the *Mirror*. 'I apologized for the thing I did wrong to the person I did it wrong to. But it would have been nice if Andrew Sachs had answered his phone, in retrospect. He would have been a good guest because then maybe the radio show would still be going if he had answered his phone, you know? No one ever mentions that side of things. They're very quick to condemn me but it isn't that hard to pick up a phone. I can't think of anything that is remotely scandalous that I have been involved in of late. I've never felt more settled.' Or happier, if his expression was anything to go by. He kept returning to the subject of having children, too, though he couldn't resist joking about

his notoriety: 'Am I now a one-woman man?' he said to the *GMTV* host Lorraine Kelly. 'Yes, I think it's true – I am in a relationship. It was a deep craving within me, Lorraine – I mistook it for lust. I thought I was promiscuous but it turns out I was just thorough – to get the right one. I'm ever so happy.' Russell was clear about one thing: his old life was well and truly in the past.

Given how serious the relationship was becoming, and despite the fact that they'd only been an item for two months, it was time for a rather more delicate introduction to take place. Meeting the parents of your beloved can be unnerving at the best of times, but when you are in an extremely high-profile relationship and have a wild past behind you, it takes on a whole new dimension. However, when Katy introduced Russell to her parents, it went well. Keith gave Russell a copy of his book, *The Cry*, designed to 'release the desperate longing for God's intervention in your life', and in response, Russell gave him *My Booky Wook*. Given that it pulled no punches about Russell's former lifestyle, it was a brave move, but it paid off.

In fact, they all got on extremely well. At the time it still wasn't widely known that Katy's parents had had wild pasts themselves, but if anyone was going to understand and accept that Russell was a changed man, it was them. Not that they were going to let him get away with any bad behaviour. 'Russell must go towards the light and not towards the darkness,' Mary said firmly. 'Only God can take the very worst person and turn them around for good. You just have to see how the Lord's will is done. I mean,

how many times have your kids disappointed you so profoundly that you wanted to get up from the chair and knock them out? There are parts of Russell's book where he's really hungry for positive influences in his life. I think the two of them are hungry. They are basically looking for God and they are seeking the truth – and they are going to find it.'

Keith was equally supportive. 'We all have a past,' he said. 'I was in the Jimi Hendrix and Janis Joplin era, and I used to take LSD. Russell's really got a hunger for the supernatural. He's got a real spiritual hunger. Russell really likes us because he has a whole new different concept on Christianity now that he has met us.'

Keith was also coming to terms with Katy's new lifestyle, which couldn't be more different to the one she'd known as a child. 'People say: "What do you think about Katy? Aren't you ashamed? Why did Katy sing that song, 'I Kissed A Girl?'" And I say, "I don't know. Why does a duck stand on one leg and go quack? I don't know." And I say, "I don't know about kissing a girl, but I kissed God and liked it better."' It was clear that he had not only come to terms with what Katy was up to, but was happy with her choice of life partner. For it was increasingly obvious that that was what Russell was going to be.

As Christmas approached, Russell jetted off to LA for a short break to be with his beloved – encountering a small problem with his passport at Customs because of his past drug issues – and speculation intensified that he was going

to propose. The fact that they'd been a couple for such a short time was neither here nor there, as both of them were convinced they'd found their other half, so why wait?

The rumours came thick and fast after that. And although newspaper reports involving famous couples often rely on a certain amount of fiction, in this particular case it was true: Russell *had* been shopping for a ring. He was also planning a pretty monumental way to propose. 'Russell is searching for a jewelry designer to make up a ring in time for New Year after the pair discussed what they wanted to have,' one of the couple's friends told Splash News. 'Russell also has the approval of Katy's parents and everyone in the pair's close circle knows about the engagement.'

That didn't stop reports linking her to Robert Pattinson, but these were so wide of the mark that Katy felt moved to tweet, 'Read a bunch of yesterday's news – BOLLOCKS. Ppl should know by now that I don't do vampires, but I do DO @rustyrockets [Brand's Twitter name].' She was clearly as smitten as her beau.

Katy also received admiring words from the boys of 3OH!3, Nathaniel Motte and Sean Matthew Foreman, who had just made a video with her. 'As we filmed with Katy I suddenly thought that this video will be ingrained and preserved in the consciousness of every teenage boy's fantasy,' Nathaniel told the *Daily Star*. 'I realized that we were frolicking with the pin-up for the 21st Century. That was slightly weird as she's our pal. We do feel like brothers to Katy and I can say that her and Russell make a very sweet couple.' An increasingly serious one, too.

As Christmas approached Russell gave his own inimit-able take on events: 'I'm going to be in church, dressed in sackcloth, whipping myself on the back for being a bad boyfriend to a good Christian girl,' he told the *Daily Star*. 'I think I'll be in Blighty. My Christmas is so traditional that I hang around in a stable worshipping a baby. I haven't got no brothers or sisters so I'll be with my mum, some of my mates and I'll see my girlfriend and in-laws.' This was actu-ally to be his last Christmas as a single man, but more than ever he gave the impression of luxuriating in his new world. That reference to the 'in-laws' was telling: the cou-ple might not yet be formally engaged, but it was only a matter of time. The pair were snapped sledging together on Hampstead Heath, and as with everything they did, they gave the impression that a moment apart was a moment wasted.

The couple were managing to enjoy themselves all over the world now. As rumours of an engagement gathered pace, they turned up in India – a surprise present from Russell to Katy after she mentioned, over a curry, that she loved Indian culture – at that ultimate monument to love, the Taj Mahal. 'He built this for me,' tweeted Katy before they got their hands decorated with henna and covered themselves in wreaths of flowers.

Russell, unrecognizable as the famed Lothario of yes-terday, decided they would usher in the New Year in a way that involved a little more than a few renditions of 'Auld Lang Syne', so he arranged for them to see a love guru. And so, as the clocks chimed in the year 2010, the couple

donned traditional Indian outfits – in Russell, Katy had found a partner who was just as interested in clothes as she was – went to a tent at the bottom of a mountain in Jaipur, and had their relationship formally blessed, as they were granted love and divine happiness.

'Russell wanted to do something special for Katy to show her how much she means to him,' a friend said at the time. 'They wanted to take part in a traditional ceremony and thought there was no better time than on New Year's Eve. The ceremony is usually used to bless new couples in the hope it might lead them toward marriage.'

They didn't need much leading. Friends leaked news to the press continually, with one telling *US Weekly* that Katy had 'never connected with anybody like this' and that Russell 'is super into her. She says he makes her laugh like nobody else in the world'. Russell texted a senior journalist on the *Sun*, saying, 'It's true. Much love.' Then he told another friend, 'Katy's managed to tame me. This is it – I'm completely in love.'

The worst-kept secret in showbusiness finally came out in early January: Katy and Russell were engaged. And when people asked what Russell had that other men didn't? Katy replied, 'A vocabulary.' The hints had been coming in thick and fast: in the February copy of *Glamour* magazine, Katy had been photographed wearing a large, heart-shaped pink ring. 'When I find a partner who is my teammate, I'm not going to play by any rules, I'm just going to go with my heart,' Katy told *Glamour*. 'Why wait? I just wrote a song [that goes], "They say it's hard to meet your match, gotta

find my other half so we can make a perfect shape."' Now it seemed she had, and after just three months.

'We can confirm Russell and Katy Perry are engaged,' said Russell's publicists. 'We were on an elephant. We were in India,' Russell later said of the proposal. 'It was mid-night. It is not a good idea to be on the back of an elephant in a fireworks display.'

Meanwhile, it was increasingly easy to see why Russell was so smitten: 'There's got to be respect,' Katy told one inter-viewer. 'For me, that's hard because it's easy for me to steamroll guys. I need a man who tells me the party's over, that it's time to go home, because we have to work in the morning.' Russell – who works considerably harder than people gave him credit for – was able to do just that. And he had beaten his addictions. 'Drugs are a huge, huge deal-breaker,' Katy went on. 'Substance abuse is also a deal-breaker.'

No date had been set for the wedding, but given the speed at which things were moving, it clearly wouldn't be far away. 'I love you,' Katy tweeted to Russell, who con-tinued to behave like a besotted teenager. The engagement ring was a giant two-carat diamond, said to be worth about £30,000, and there was even speculation that Katy was pregnant, which she fuelled by tweeting, 'Let me tell you 2010 is BUMPIN!' Katy tweeted of her beloved. 'That boy is a monster . . .' There wasn't too much doubt about what she meant.

In early January, Katy made a return to the studios – she did, after all, have a career to attend to. She answered phones at the Haiti telethon, before performing at the

Haze nightclub in Las Vegas's Aria Resort. Meanwhile Russell was with her in California, having firmly based himself in LA, and while the two weren't officially living together, mainly out of respect for Katy's parents, they were constantly at one another's side.

Katy also appeared as a judge on *American Idol*, alongside Avril Lavigne and the regular crew, where she managed to make her mark. 'I've always been a brutally honest type of gal,' she told Ryan Seacrest before the show began. 'People are going to get the best advice that they need to hear.' So were the other judges: 'Don't ever put someone through because you feel bad,' she informed Kara Dio-Guardi when Kara wanted to let someone through and Katy disagreed.

'What happened to girl power?' Kara asked Katy before mocking 'I Kissed A Girl'.

'I'm going to have to throw my Coke in your face,' Katy replied.

It certainly livened up the show, as did the (male) contestant who offered to have sex with Simon Cowell, to which Katy responded, 'I feel dirty and it takes a lot for me to feel dirty.'

While Katy continued to be massively in demand – she'd even been signed up as the face of acne cream Proactiv – Russell was rumoured to have bought a house.

Russell had always used his life for comic material, leading to misunderstandings from time to time when jokes he made about life with Katy were taken too seriously. Stand-up was no longer the major part of his life it once had

been, but he still did the odd gig from time to time, and his new life featured in these performances. In one such appearance at the Upright Citizens Brigade theatre in Hollywood, he talked about his cat Morrissey and Katy's cat Kitty Purry: 'I love my cat so it's very traumatic,' he explained. 'Morrissey hates living with the other one and I don't know what to do. I feel like I've betrayed his genitals with monogamy. No one knows who I am over here and I'm fine with that, but going out with someone who is more famous means I'm the cameraman.'

It was an extremely good-natured remark, and one that provided another key to their happiness: Russell was genuinely happy to let Katy run the show. He was so happy being with her that he didn't feel the need to compete when it came to their careers; the fact that he was nine years older than her helped too. As for the cats – well, it did rather give the game away about them living together.

Even so, Russell could – and did – act up. In the run-up to the Clive Davis party before the Grammy awards, he rather forgot himself: 'Sorry, I thought this was a Clive Dunn event. I thought we'd be here talking about *Dad's Army*. I've been misled,' he said. Clive Dunn had starred in *Dad's Army*, but almost no one in the States had a clue who he was or what *Dad's Army* was. Matters weren't helped when Russell started singing the show's theme tune, 'Who Do You Think You Are Kidding Mr Hitler?', which elicited a few shocked laughs. Nor was that all: 'Grammys . . . I know why it's called that. That's how much coke you need to cope with it.'

'Stop it and behave!' said Katy, who didn't know whether to laugh or be annoyed. 'I don't want to upset the Grammys, I want one.' Russell behaved, but still Katy didn't get an award that year. There was plenty of time for that, though.

As her relationship with Russell matured, so did Katy. She was a woman now, about to be married, and as a result she was growing up in ways she'd never needed to before, and it was affecting not only her life, but also her appearance, which remained very important to her. Katy is a serious style icon, who's as revered for her fashion sense as for her music, and all that was changing and developing.

'Some of the kid shit I've grown out of completely,' she said in an interview with *Nylon* magazine. 'I'm taking it out on the Shirley Temple, Betty Boop, Lichtenstein kind of thing. It's still fun, but a bit darker. It's not as annoying. Sometimes, I feel like a big strawberry with a face on it. Sometimes I really feel like I'm more of a Taylor Swift. Love has really affected my songwriting. I know how to handle a man now.' In truth, she always had done, but then Russell was more of a handful than most men.

Teenage Dreaming

As news of the engagement spread, the curiosity surrounding Katy and Russell's relationship intensified. That they were both blissfully happy was self-evident, but it really did seem to be a case of opposites attracting. Both felt they had met their match. Katy might have tamed Russell, but she had found a man who wouldn't let her get away with any nonsense either: 'He's good for me,' she told *Nylon*. 'He calls the shots. But I like that. I've been waiting for someone I couldn't steamroll.' And it seemed that Russell couldn't steamroll her either.

Katy was managing to keep her phenomenally successful career and her romantic life going while another major event drew near. Before she got married, she was due to release her second mainstream album, *Teenage Dream*, and it was crucial that the release was handled properly. An artist's second album is almost more important than the first, for it's an indication of whether or not they'll have staying power. There are many singers who achieve one big success but never manage to recapture that, and Katy had to prove she wasn't one of them. If her second album didn't do well, at least she'd made some money and met Russell. Musically, however, she'd be back to square one.

And so began Katy's big schmooze-fest. Glittering

soirées for senior record company executives were thrown across America. Michael Pallen, director of the major Chicago-based digital entertainment company VerveLife, was present at one, and his account illustrates the fact that if Katy was nervous, she hid it well. Quite as charming as ever, she held court and enthralled those around her.

'A few months prior to the release of Katy Perry's sophomore album, EMI threw the pop star a CD listening party,' Michael recalls. 'Held in one of the fancy suites of the Trump Tower in Chicago, Illinois, the party filled the room with radio personalities, music professionals, and loads of candy, including a cake made of Skittles to match the theme of her new album. It felt like we were walking into Candyland. With the Chicago El-train tracks behind her, Miss Perry sipped on her vodka drink as her new songs were played for the audience for the first time. In between songs, the petite Perry, who was dressed in a cute little black dress and had her hair up in a sexy pony tail, discussed the meaning behind each song and her excitement for this album.

'After songs like "Firework", "Peacock", "Teenage Dream" and "California Gurls" were previewed, Katy took the time to individually meet everyone and snap a few photos. As both me and my wife approached Katy, she greeted us both with a big hug. We snapped a few photos and then she began talking with us like we were best friends. We talked about my recent wedding. She asked my wife to see her wedding ring. They discussed her ring choice. She asked how wedding planning was and if we had a wedding

planner. (We told Katy we did everything on our own and she pretty much had a heart attack. She was like, "There is no way I can do this on my own, so I am going to have a planner.") Katy was a few months away from marrying actor/comedian Russell Brand, so you could tell she was getting excited about her wedding.

'Throughout the whole time, Katy had the biggest beautiful smile on her face. In magazines and in her videos, she is gorgeous. In person, she is stunning. To compliment her beauty, Katy is a genuinely nice person. Not at one moment did I feel like she didn't want to speak with us. She seemed to really enjoy meeting us and talking with us.'

If anything explains Katy's popularity, it's this. Despite her fame, she hasn't developed airs and graces and is careful to treat everyone around her with respect. It's both charming and professional, the mark of a genuinely decent character as well as someone who understands the importance of getting on with people.

As Katy worked the circuit, she was never far away from being reminded of the dark side of fame, however. One of the biggest problems faced by many celebrities is the advent of a stalker, and suddenly Katy found herself with just such a problem. A woman, seemingly obsessed with Katy and Russell, had started posting strange messages on Twitter: 'You need to dump that fucking asshole Russell, he is shit,' was a typical post. 'There's nothing good about that fucker, he's not funny, he doesn't give a fuck about you. Dump his ass, Katy. Please!'

Not only was it unpleasant, it was patently untrue. But

what could Katy do? It went with the territory, and in these days of constant surveillance, when anyone with a mobile phone can turn paparazzo, twenty-four-hour exposure is an accepted fact of life. There was almost nowhere in the world where Katy could be anonymous, making security not only necessary but part of her everyday life.

Another necessary evil to be endured was the constant – and usually untrue – gossip. Still unable to believe that Russell Brand was settling down, stories would periodically circulate that all was not well between the couple and that the wedding was off. At a pre-Oscar party Russell was seen laughing with a woman and twanging her fishnets: it was totally innocent but still it sent the rumour mill into overdrive. (Katy, incidentally, was present at the time.) The fact that they both had careers to pursue – Russell was promoting *Get Me to the Greek* – meant that they couldn't spend all their time together, but when one of them was spotted out alone, no matter how innocent the reason, tongues wagged. Both of them just had to get on with it: there was no point in issuing a continual stream of denials, as they would be never-ending, but it was another unwelcome facet of Katy's fame.

In the end the stalking turned very nasty, with more than 100 posts a day, some demanding that Russell should kill himself. Katy eventually snapped. 'Hey, can you please stop being so disrespectful? It's not cool,' she said, but to no avail. This was another problem with being a celebrity in the modern age: accessibility. Today's stars have to tweet and engage with their fans.

At the Nickelodeon Kids' Choice Awards in LA, Katy showed she was game for a laugh by submitting to being gunged with good grace – she opened a box to have green slime shoot out at her – then a matter of hours later she appeared in full goddess mode, dressed in a red leotard and riding on an elephant, for a party for Perez Hilton where she was due to sing 'Happy Birthday'. The party had a circus theme and others stars present included Mel B as the ringmaster, and Leona Lewis as a trapeze artist. Perez, naturally, was in his element, the excited belle of the ball.

To the amusement of those who'd known him in the old days, Russell was spotted starting martial arts training. It was claimed he wanted to build up his frame in the run-up to the wedding, but the fact of the matter was that Russell was becoming a Hollywood star now, so like Katy he had to consider his career, and in Hollywood, leading men were expected to have muscles. The couple were working hard in every way possible, although the wedding planning, complete with planner, continued to surge ahead.

'I think the wedding will be small,' said Katy, although in the event it was anything but. 'I always have a ton of people around me and I think the people that are going to share this moment with us are the people we want to integrate into each other's lives. We don't necessarily want it to be a drunk fest of people just, you know, one night and then forgetting about it. We want it to be about the love.' In the end it was about that, but in quite spectacular style.

Russell was a growing phenomenon in the States at this

time, and when he gave an interview to *Playboy* in the summer of 2010, it gave a great insight into how much his life had changed. Monogamy was clearly a revelation. 'When I was at my most promiscuous I was like a charging locomotive,' he said. 'I had a team of experts who took care of finding women for me. They had very specific instructions. It was as if I was talking to a wine steward, "I'm looking for something French, a bit fruity, smells of oak." [But] the majority of people in sex rehab are just disgusting men.' He was so over that, he could have added. Russell couldn't avoid stirring it a little wherever he went, but he had clearly calmed down. 'It was nice to have sex with loads and loads of people,' he said. 'But my life has changed. I have not cheated on Katy. I have not got off with other birds.'

In May, two announcements came out in quick succession: that Katy's next album would be released in August and that the happy couple would be getting married in October, with Goa being a likely location for the nuptials. Russell couldn't resist teasing there, too: 'Of course we're going to have a child some day,' he told the *Daily Express*. 'I'm hoping for a hybrid creature, something from Greek mythology like a satyr. It's [the wedding] going to be indulgent, right? Everyone's going to be topless, the bride, the groom – that's me – our parents, all topless. It will be a festival of decadence. The first thing we're going to do is slaughter a swan. That's to the god Zeus. Our wedding is essentially going to be a recreation of the greatest moments in mythological history.' Was he having a laugh? Yes.

In actual fact, according to his bride-to-be, Russell was genuinely excited about the wedding plans. Being such a flamboyant creature he could hardly be otherwise, and given how much his life had changed, he clearly wanted to make that point in some style. 'He is like a groomzilla,' said Katy. 'Totally into it. Frankly insane about it all. We go out for breakfast and he has to stop at a newsstand and get one of those glossy bridal magazines. Then all through breakfast he's talking about colours, dress designs and even designing the monograms we want. He is way over his head with excitement about it all.'

There had been a good deal of speculation about how Katy's parents felt in the run-up to the happy event, but according to Russell they were delighted. 'They're like refugees from the 60s,' he told the *Guardian*. 'They're really spiritual, take their religion seriously, but also he did a lot of acid, her dad. He was born-again as a result of being almost on the point of vagrancy. Katy's mother went to Berkeley in San Francisco and went to a Doors gig and danced with Jimi Hendrix. They're not austerely judging me like Quakers. They really like me. Her dad gets me cute presents. A teddy bear, bearing the legend "When Did My Wild Oats Turn To All Bran?"' Katy's parents clearly had the measure of Russell and weren't alarmed at all.

As the release of Katy's second album drew nearer, she and her record company worked hard to create that all-important buzz. Apart from schmoozing within the industry, Katy was beginning to talk to journalists, dropping hints about what was to come. The music press were

also getting previews, with Katy coyly telling the *Daily Star*, which had been invited to a listening party in LA, 'I've had a bit of a British influence in my life.' This was no bad thing when Britain is considered a leading contender in the music industry, and nor did it hurt that some of the numbers could quite clearly be linked to Katy's personal life.

'Circle The Drain' was a case in point. 'People will think it's about Travis but it could be about many other different situations,' said Katy. '"Circle The Drain" is intense – it's my Alanis Morissette's "You Oughta Know". It has the F-word in it five times, but I don't think it's me shocking people – you always say fuck when it's called for.'

If it was about Travis, who was now being quite open about his addictions, it certainly explained why drugs were such a deal-breaker for Katy. The song lashed out at drug users: 'You could have been the greatest/But you'd rather get wasted.' Whatever Katy said about it not necessarily being about Travis, it explained a great deal.

'Some of the stuff I played tonight is a bit sugary sweet but when you listen to the record head to toe I think it's completely appetizing,' she continued. 'I didn't want to have just club songs. People are living real lives, working jobs, having relationships. There's definitely a bit more substance and perspective on this record.'

Russell, of course, had also been an influence, although Katy was adamant that 'Peacock' was not about him. 'I'm a big fan of innuendo and puns,' Katy said. '"Peacock" is fun, but it could be totally dirty. A five-year-old could sing it, but your fifteen-year-old will know what it means. My

Russell songs are more romantic – such as "Not Like The Movies". Sometimes we girls are like: "He's the one," but deep down there's that little scratch. There's no scratch at this moment, which is fantastic. When you know, you know.' As it happens, though, the critics loathed the song.

The smitten couple just couldn't stop telling people how loved up they were. Every time either of them opened their mouth it was to utter a new protestation of love – understandable, perhaps, in the run-up to their wedding, but it was a huge break from at least one of their pasts. Russell, in particular, couldn't stop talking about how much he'd changed. 'I used to treat women badly but I'm really trying my best,' he told the *Sunday Mirror*. 'There's no lying or tricking. It's a nice feeling. I'm quite able, I think, to seduce people . . . but with Katy – I mean I love her, in a really pure way. She's a beautiful person, funny and gentle and sweet. But she's so demanding. A lot of the time, it's mental. She's a proper handful. It's very diverting. It's easy to be an arsehole, but now I've a woman who won't tolerate it.' Which was, of course, the reason he had chosen her.

They were so in love, it seemed, that they couldn't even bear to have dressing rooms too far apart. At the MTV Music Awards in the Universal Studios Gibson Amphitheater in Los Angeles, they managed to get rooms next door to each other, and there was much flitting between the two. Katy was very much on duty that night – amongst numerous costume changes, she was performing her new single 'California Gurls' – but their flirting was so incessant

that they were constantly on Twitter. Russell started by saying that he hoped his album from *Get Me to the Greek* would make him a 'pretend poster' [sic].

'Pretend poostar?' tweeted Katy.

'Because you're a genuine poostar!' tweeted Russell. 'Ha, so the hunter has become the hunted. Sorry. I'll sleep on the couch.' The wit might not have been Wildean, but there was no denying the love.

Despite all the trappings of her new life, however, Katy was still the nice girl she had always been. One of her biggest rivals, Lady Gaga, had just made a video for her single 'Alejandro', which featured her dressed as a nun in a red PVC habit, swallowing rosary beads and generally disporting herself in a manner not unfamiliar to fans of Madonna, but which wouldn't go down well with the Catholic church. Katy, while not Catholic herself, was disgusted. 'Using blasphemy as entertainment is as cheap as a comedian telling a fart joke,' she tweeted, and she remained unamused whenever confronted by a slight against Christianity, even when uttered by her husband-to-be. As Travis had pointed out, Katy hadn't really changed that much, though what Travis failed to understand is that this fact went down well with Russell. However bohemian a figure he cut, what he really wanted was a good old-fashioned girl.

That didn't stop Russell from making risqué remarks, though. He gave an interview with *Rolling Stone* in which he confessed to giving himself a helping hand during long absences from Katy, adding, 'Going on a voyage of self-

discovery isn't as exciting as getting your cock sucked while chomping on chocolate and playing Nintendo, is it?' Katy and her parents wisely stayed silent, but it prompted some enraged outbursts from Keith's churchgoers, who didn't want to be named: 'Like everyone else here, they have to be appalled at his gutter comments,' one fumed. 'Some are clearly tongue-in-cheek efforts at humour and not to be taken seriously. But impressionable teenagers who obviously hear and read what he says are going to think it must be OK to talk like that if a Hollywood star does. I can tell you Mr Brand is not going to get a warm welcome from many quarters if he turns up here with Katy. It wouldn't surprise me if her parents suggest they get married elsewhere.' Not that there was much evidence that Katy's parents were having a great deal of say when it came to the wedding, as the bride and groom seemed to be making all the plans.

As 'California Gurls' was released, the promotional merry-go-round began and Katy started country-hopping again. Originally called 'California Girls', the title was changed as a tribute to Big Star, who had just lost one of their members, referring to their number 'September Gurls'. The song was actually leaked online, so Capitol Records brought forward the release date of the track, which had been produced by Dr Luke, Max Martin and Benny Blanco and featured the rapper Snoop Dogg. According to Katy, it was a response to Jay-Z's 'Empire State Of Mind', which was about New York.

'It's so great that "Empire State Of Mind" is huge and that everybody has the New York song, but what the fuck?' she told *Rolling Stone*. 'What about LA? What about California? And it's been a minute since we've had a California song and especially from a girl's perspective. We took the references of Prince, which is always a great reference, and we took a lot of the '90s . . . almost that house music, some of those references.' There were, however, rumours about some trouble with the Beach Boys, whose Sixties hit 'California Girls' had been one of the most successful singles ever released, on the grounds that Snoop Dogg ends the record by rapping, 'I wish you all could be California girls'. This seemed to be a direct reference to the Beach Boys' track, and there were reports that they were going to sue. In the event, nothing of the sort took place: Beach Boys member Mike Love, one of the co-writers, along with Brian Wilson, of the original song said, 'The Beach Boys are definitely not suing Katy Perry; in fact we are flattered that her fantastically successful song is bringing to mind to millions of people our 1965 recording of the Beach Boys' "California Girls". We think her song is great and wish her all the success in the world.'

The song was indeed a massive success, giving Katy her second No 1 and Snoop Dogg his third, as well as receiving a thumbs-up from the critics. '"Gurls" is a big, bright, decidedly beach-friendly pop tune, full of sunshiney synthesizers, starry, electronic whooshes and loose, funky, wah-wah guitar flourishes,' wrote James Montgomery on MTV's website. 'As if all that weren't enough to guarantee

it instant summer-jam success, well, then wait until you hear the positively massive chorus, on which Perry sings about Daisy Dukes-wearing California gurls ... Oh, and Snoop Dogg also shows up midway through to contribute a verse dedicated to the "toned, tanned, fit and ready" Cali girls he loves.'

In *USA Today*, Steve Jones and Edna Gunderson called it 'an effervescent toast to summer fun'. Nick Levine on Digital Spy said, 'It slips lyrics about "sippin' gin and juice", "laying underneath the palm trees" and, erm, "sex on the beach" over a snappy electropop backing that brings to mind Calvin Harris grinding against Ke$ha in a '90s super-club. Not only does it name-check Snoop Doggy Dogg, but it gives him an entire verse to drool over the gurls of the Golden State. The result? As classy as the titular hero-ines' outfit of choice ... but, thanks to an unstoppable pop chorus and Perry's charismatic vocals, just as easy to fall for. We mean, like, totally head over stilettos.'

The video, directed by Matthew Cullen, was pure Katy. Inspired by *Alice in Wonderland*, Katy remarked that it was 'something to watch when you have the munchies – it's all edible'. She wasn't joking. She had, on various occasions in the past, dived into cakes, ending up with sponge and cream everywhere, but this video took the idea to a whole new extreme. Based in 'Candyfornia', the set is decorated with cupcakes, ice-cream, cotton candy and lollipops.

'We named it Candyfornia instead of California, so it's a different world,' Katy told MTV. 'It's not just like, "Oh, let's go to the beach and throw a party and then shoot a

music video!" It's more like, "Let's put us California Gurls in a whole different world!" The boys always dream about dating a California Gurl . . . just because we've got the sun shining 365 days a year. And I love New York girls. I think they're hot, and I think they have a lot of attitude. But I'm telling you, when it comes wintertime, they're all gonna be singing "California Gurls".' Her optimism was not misplaced.

The plot, such as it was, involved various 'Queens of Candyfornia' being held captive by Snoop using various candy-related devices: Katy frees them all and they dance on the beach before engaging in a war with Snoop, which they win. Visually it was spectacular, with vast numbers of costume changes, a near naked Katy lying atop the clouds and a novel take on Lady Gaga's bra-gun, where Katy affixes whipped cream canisters to her embonpoint and demolishes the enemy. Snoop, clad in a suit covered in ice-cream cones and seeming to play the characters on a board game before he joins them, looks on in seventh heaven, as well he might.

It was noticeable that Katy was gradually becoming more daring with her look. The cover of 'California Gurls' features her in a retro bikini, while the succession of cup-cake-decorated tops she wears in the video only accentuate her décolletage. The near-naked shot, floating on the clouds, was replicated on the cover of the album, but the feel was still naughty but nice, rather than anything more sensational. *Teenage Dream* was a huge success, peaking at No 1 in the charts and becoming the ninth album in the history

of the charts to have spawned four No 1 singles, 'California Gurls' being the first. It had been a great deal of hard work: 'I'd wake up, go to the gym, go home, go to the studio, come home, wake up and do it all over again. I'd do that every day besides Sunday, the Lord's day – day of rest,' Katy said.

Unsurprisingly, a great deal of planning had gone into it all, with Katy and her team aiming the album squarely at her core target market: teenagers. Katy realized how important it was for her career, too. 'The second record is really important to me because I think it shows whether I'm meant to do this, or I got lucky,' she told *Rolling Stone*. 'Basically, what I want to do is not alienate the audience that I have at all. I think some people feel like they have had success with one thing and one idea and one record and they want to pull a 180 and try a totally different thing. I definitely feel like that's the wrong move. I feel like you just have to grow from it, you can branch off of it but keep the tree the same in some ways. Some people get full of themselves, and they think that anything they do is going to work or turn to gold or be the right move, and the reason why you're here is because of the people that like your music and the fans, so you always should keep an ear open to what they're saying.'

It was a sensible strategy. Katy was working with the best in the business, including Dr Luke, Greg Wells, Guy Sigsworth, Max Martin, Ryan Tedder, Rivers Cuomo, Thaddis Harrell, Greg Kurstin, Benny Blanco, Darkchild, Cathy Dennis, Ester Dean, The-Dream and Christopher 'Tricky'

Stewart. 'It's so exciting,' Katy told MTV. 'It's coming out this summer. It's a summer record. It's what I said I wanted earlier. We nailed it. It's roller-skating. It's '90s. It's Ace of Base. It's Cyndi Lauper. It's like all these colors and more . . . There might be some really cool guest appearances by some cool rappers from the West Coast [Snoop Dog and Kanye West both appear on the album]. I mean, you'll just have to see, since I'm a California girl, you know. And then some best friends might be appearing . . . We'll see! It's going to be fun. It's going to be one of those records that is everybody's favorite guilty pleasure.'

The appearance of the artwork, the accompanying video and the general look of *Teenage Dreams* was very important too, as a reflection of the development of Katy's own style. 'It's like going from Shirley Temple, Betty Boop to more of a Betty Paige, pop-art-sarcastic-fun-Lichtenstein picture: still bright, but the colors are more saturated, and it's more metallic fuchsia or purple than bubblegum pink,' she said. It was certainly extremely striking, with Katy wearing different brightly coloured wigs to promote the tracks, along with a succession of attractive outfits.

The album got a mixed reaction, but on the whole the critics liked it. 'Beneath the fruity outfits and fart jokes, Perry is clearly serious about the business of hit songcraft; that doesn't make *Dream* nearly cohesive as an album, but it does provide, intermittently, exactly the kind of high-fructose rush she's aiming for,' said Leah Greenblatt in *Entertainment Weekly*. Rob Sheffield in *Rolling Stone* said it was 'an all-American teen-pop sound that's older than the

Hollywood Hills'. Matthew Cole on website Slant magazine, however, hated it: 'On her latest release, she finds humor in drunken make-out sessions and single-entendre sex talk, finds that being a celebrity isn't always a walk in the Candyland porno park, and through it all, finds maybe two or three songs to justify her album's existence,' he snapped.

The song Cole hated most – and he was not alone: even Katy's admirers were unsure about this one – was 'Peacock'. 'It's hard to imagine a song crasser or more aggravating than "Peacock",' he said. 'Every review of *Teenage Dream* will mention this track, and that's because it's potentially historic in its badness, to the point that, once you've heard it, you too will have to describe it to other people just to convince yourself that it really exists. The short of it is that Perry wants to see some guy's peacock, and by peacock, she, of course, means penis; she says the word "cock" somewhere around 100 times . . . It's one of those viscerally embarrassing musical moments where you start to feel ashamed of yourself just for witnessing it.'

It was an exceptionally harsh judgement, but he wasn't alone: an awful lot of people hated 'Peacock', and the fact that Russell was thought to be the inspiration – despite Katy's denials – didn't help. It didn't really matter, though. The album did what it had to, establishing Katy as a serious contender who was in it for the long haul. Three more tracks from the album, 'Teenage Dream', 'Firework' and 'E.T.' (featuring Kanye West) all went on to become No 1s,

and the album itself sold in millions. Katy's own teenage dream had finally come true: she was the star she'd always wanted to be.

But that wasn't all that was going on in her life – because Katy had a wedding to plan.

Growing Pains

Although the wedding was getting near, Katy and Russell were forced to spend a lot of time apart. Katy was promoting her new album heavily, while Russell had started work on a remake of the film *Arthur*. Russell was based in New York, while Katy was everywhere. She appeared as a guest judge on *The X Factor* – one of many celebrities to do so – while the regular host, Dannii Minogue, was away on maternity leave, and returned to the show a couple of months later to perform 'Firework'. In between times she was in Kuala Lumpur, in Malaysia, for the MTV World Stage Live, then it was off to LA to host the Teen Choice Awards. There was scarcely time to breathe.

When they were together, however, they were as happy as ever. 'Living with Russell is like an episode of "I Love Lucy", with two Lucys in the house,' Katy told the *Daily Star*. 'It's hard to cope with his humour but he's fun and I love hanging out with him. That's why we are getting married. He introduced me to Oscar Wilde and Morrissey and I introduced him to kittens.'

Still, the promotional work continued. As the wedding planners did their thing in the background, Katy flew across Europe, looking demure in France and channelling

Marilyn Monroe in Germany before straddling a giant rocket! It was all becoming a blur.

She was branching out in other ways, too, as the voice of a female Smurf in the forthcoming animated movie *The Smurfs*. Because of her sheltered background, Katy hadn't seen the original television series, so she was making up for lost time. 'I'm Smurfette,' she told the *Daily Record*. 'I love the idea of being a cartoon and animation. It's funny because I was never allowed to watch *The Smurfs* growing up. My mom thought that Smurfette being the only female in the village was a little bit scantily clad, if you know what I mean. I grew up in a very sheltered house. But this *Smurfs* is definitely one for the kids. It is not one of those movies that has to work on so many different levels. It is a family movie. They [the producers] were just listening [to one of Katy's records] and not really knowing who was who and they just liked the texture of my voice. So now I am Smur-falicious.'

When asked how it was, being a cartoon, Katy replied, 'You have to do the script a few times but it wasn't tough, not for me,' said Katy, whose stage persona is pretty car-toonish in itself. 'I always feel like a cartoon on a pretty frequent basis, when I'm dressing up, and especially on stage. So I think it was just natural.' Clearly, it was the per-fect mix.

As Katy's star rose ever higher, it seemed like everyone wanted a piece of her. That meant lots of promotional opportunities, so in the autumn of 2010, she announced plans to launch her own perfume, entitled Purr. 'I kept

wanting to tell someone!' Katy told MTV when the news broke. 'It wasn't just like, "I love gardenias." That would have been the easy route. I really wanted to develop a scent that was completely unlike anything I'd smelled before and not one that smelled like a knockoff of another scent. All things edible for me are also intriguing. So if there are little dancing strawberries, I will be happy. Peppermint is cute; cotton candy is adorable. We like to keep it cute and classy. I am a product whore. I am a consumer of a multitude of beauty products and I'm always looking for the next great thing.'

It made a great deal of commercial sense. The world of celebrity perfumes is an extremely lucrative one that had the potential to increase Katy's already growing bank balance enormously. The scent, including notes of peach nectar, apple and green bamboo, as well as freesia, Bulgarian rose and vanilla orchid, was to be sold in a cat-shaped bottle – it was all very Katy, who is very feminine herself, wears catsuits onstage and, of course, has a pet cat called Kitty Purry.

'I have about 50 fragrances and I'm intrigued by the mystique scent has,' Katy told *Women's Wear Daily*. 'I saw a lot of my peers getting into this world, and, as with my music, I thought I could bring my touch to the category and make it competitive. I'm a very lyrical-based person, and the whole "purr" thing kept coming back – [the sound is in] perfume, perfect, even Perry if you say it a certain way.'

But as good as all this was for her income and profile, it

was going to take a lot of work – all of which would take her away from Russell. The couple wouldn't have been human if they hadn't felt the strain and it was evidently taking its toll when they were involved in a nasty scuffle at Los Angeles airport. Katy and Russell were heading towards the security area when photographers appeared and a fight broke out. The problem seemed to be that Russell thought they were trying to take a picture looking up Katy's skirt: he lashed out to stop them and ended up being the subject of a citizen's arrest. In the end he was taken into custody on an assault charge and accused of attacking a member of the paparazzi.

'Russell appeared to be angry the moment he saw the waiting photographers and barged past them in an obvious huff,' a witness told the *Sunday Express*. 'Everyone seemed to be jostling each other but I saw him go after this one guy in particular. He appeared to kick him, then tried to barge him with an elbow. I don't know what triggered it all but the photographer stood his ground and there was an enormous shouting match between him, Brand and three or four other photographers until the police arrived. It really was a disgraceful exhibition. Katy stood there, saying very little, but it was clear from the expression on her face that she was terrified.'

Katy was also totally supportive of her man. 'If you cross the line and try and put a lens up my dress, my fiancé will do his job and protect me,' she tweeted later in the day, and in truth it was hard not to feel sympathy for the pair. Russell was later interviewed by Jeremy Paxman

and asked what the difference was between leaving vulgar messages on the answerphone of an elderly man and shoving a camera up someone's skirt and the answer, too lengthy to be repeated here, boiled down to malice afore-thought. Russell had overstepped the mark, there was no doubt about that, but he had done so in the heat of the moment, inflamed by paparazzi trying to get a comprom-ising shot of Katy, and in the end, the charges were dropped.

Next stop was Katy's hen night, which, by all accounts, was a pretty wild party at the Hard Rock Hotel in Las Vegas, organized by Rihanna. They started with drinks by the pool before the girls went to watch Cirque du Soleil at a nearby hotel, after which they were pictured with the per-formers. Katy was fetchingly dressed in a black sequined minidress and high heels, and she was wearing a hat with 'bride' printed on it and a veil cascading down. She was also presented with a cake bearing a rather saucy adult message on top. 'I have to come up with something cool because she's getting married in India,' Rihanna had told radio DJ Ryan Seacrest earlier. 'So I'm like "Okay, now what do I do to match that?"'

Russell also had a stag do, although his was a rather more sedate affair. Accompanied by friends, including Jona-than Ross and Noel Gallagher, they started the evening promisingly enough in Peter Stringfellow's table-dancing club Angels, but given that Russell no longer drank, every-one was on their best behaviour and the night wound up in the library of the Grove Hotel in Hertfordshire – it

seemed Russell was more absorbed in his bride-to-be than anything else.

Even though the wedding was drawing closer, still the work continued. Katy recorded an episode of *The Simpsons, The Fight Before Christmas*, to be broadcast in December that year, while Russell published his second volume of memoirs, *My Booky Wook 2* (and then announced he wouldn't be writing a third as his life was going to be so quiet from now on). Not that he regretted his new life for one second: 'I used to think girls were the lucky ones for bedding me,' he told Paul O'Grady. 'Now I know I'm the lucky one to have found Katy.'

Katy was also doing the chat-show circuit, in her case appearing on *Alan Carr: Chatty Man*, where she seemed equally keen to show how much her and Russell's lives were linked: 'One of the first things I'll do [after the wedding] is apply for dual citizenship,' she said. 'I'm not too sure if I have to take a test as I've not had time to look into it, but England is like my second home. I can just pass through customs real quick. You've already kind of adopted me so maybe I don't have to go through all the paperwork?'

She wasn't joking. Katy seemed to be taking the fact that she was marrying a Brit very seriously. At the time of the June 2010 World Cup, when England was playing the United States, Katy appeared on *James Corden's World Cup Live* wearing a specially made PVC dress that combined the American and British flags, a tactful choice of outfit that suggested that, despite her outspoken image, she knew

when to be diplomatic when necessary. The dress nearly didn't arrive on time as the flight it was on was delayed: 'Another amazing race for a dress has happen [sic] again,' Katy tweeted beforehand. 'Important dress. It's on a plane now, but plane had 2 emergency stop cuz someone passed away mid flight! So sad! So we'll see if the dress makes it in time . . . If not, my world cup convo is gonna take a beating on the chat show.'

In the event there was a 1–1 draw, which for Katy, at least, was perfect: 'EVERYBODY WINS!!!' she tweeted. 'I LIKE THAT! (Plus as an american marrying a englishman . . . I am DIVIDED.)'

Their relentless work schedules were only due to ease up around the time of the nuptials, so time together beforehand was a rare commodity. However, the duo were rumoured to have come up with a solution, although as a result they would be forced to endure a huge amount of speculation about the state of their relationship. According to some reports, they decided that, with only a short time left before the big day, they'd have couples therapy to make sure that the bond between them remained strong despite spending so much time apart.

'They've been spending more time apart than ever before,' a friend of the couple told the *Daily Mirror*. 'Russell's doing 14-hour days on the *Arthur* set in New York, while Katy's been in Europe and Australia working all sorts of hours. Combine this with the time differences and, as you can imagine, it's been tough. Relationship counselling was Katy's idea because she was adamant they

should make their relationship rock solid. As a result they both clear an hour in their schedules every day to have a conference call with a therapist, talking things over and making their bond as watertight as possible. Now they are getting married, Katy didn't feel comfortable with the amount of girls who knew where Russell lived – and of course the history it carries.'

Almost immediately rumours arose that all might not be well between them, but people seemed to be entirely missing the point. For a start, Katy's from California, a place where it's perfectly normal to have therapy even when nothing is wrong. Second, it was practical. Katy's not an idiot: she realized that as two major stars they had their own careers to pursue and that if they wanted to make things work between them, they would have to make a little extra effort. Russell realized it too. Neither of them wanted to risk growing apart, so they were doing everything they could to prevent problems emerging in the first place. It was an utterly practical, sensible decision.

The pair also had a new kitten to add to their menagerie of Morrissey and Kitty Purry. 'We have a new kitten called Krusty,' Katy told the *Daily Record*. 'We came up with it because it's Katy and Rusty [Russell's nickname] – so we crushed them together because we are very narcissistic and made Krusty.

'She's only eight weeks old but she is so annoying and a lot of work. She is jumping on top of my head at 3am and pissing in the bed and pooping in the bed. The whole works. Kids? Ugh. This is a child, so I don't know if I can

handle it right yet. We have three cats. If we get any more, I will be the cat lady. But she is usually the one that wakes us up. And we are in the middle of a really hectic time but we work out times to see each other.' Clearly they were just about managing to have a domestic life and getting a new pet was a sure sign that they were determined to make the relationship work.

Whatever the truth of it, Katy seemed determined to make an outward show of her devotion. At the MTV Video Music Awards in September 2010, Katy turned up in a stylish black and white Marchesa frock, comprising a white skirt and nude-coloured top overlaid with black embroidery, Jimmy Choos, rainbow-coloured highlights in her hair and an extraordinary manicure, which featured different pictures of Russell on every nail. Opinion was divided over various aspects of the outfit: some thought the manicure an adorable tribute to her beloved, while others found it a little OTT; the dress, a sweet shape, was also, in Katy's words, somewhat akin to a figure-skating outfit.

Katy was there to present Best Male Video – Eminem won for 'Not Afraid' – and she was also up for two awards herself. One was Best Female Video for 'California Gurls', and the other was for Best Pop Video for the same song, although in the event she lost out on both awards to Lady Gaga's 'Bad Romance'. It didn't matter, though, as the evening was an anniversary of sorts, since it was a year since she and Russell had got together at the 2009 VMAs.

Katy's second single from the album was the title song,

'Teenage Dream'. Written by Katy and Bonnie McKee, alongside Max Martin, Katy described the song as a 'pure' moment for her, one in which she was able to look back on her own teenage years as she got ready for her wedding. Various early versions were rejected by Dr Luke and the girls were finally shown 'Homecoming', a 2007 single by The Teenagers, and asked to come up with something similar. At the time the women felt a little discouraged.

'Katy and I wrote and rewrote the song four times; we wanted a "forever young" type of feel,' Bonnie said in an interview with Alex Kazemi. 'Katy started with a lyric about Peter Pan that was cool, but it just kept feeling too young. We wanted it to have more edge, more sex. There was a version that included the line, "and the next thing you know, you're a mom in a minivan." It kept us laughing uncontrollably for an hour. We literally wrote it beginning to end three times while rolling around the studio floor delirious. Finally, we thought we had cracked the code. We wrote something that was based on the metaphor of "trying me on", comparing the feeling of wearing new clothes to sex, kind of a "Dress You Up In My Love" deal. We swore we had it, then Benny Blanco came in, he was like, "Uh, no." Luke always makes us "Benny Proof" everything. He says that if Benny doesn't get it, America won't get it.

'Katy and I looked at each other in dismay, knowing we would have to start all over again . . . I really wanted to bring my best, so I took it home and sat with it. I thought about my adolescent years, my first love. I thought about watch-

ing Baz Luhrmann's *Romeo + Juliet*, putting on a mini disco ball, and just dreaming of Leo. I thought about my friends and I having slumber parties in the 90s, giddy at the mere thought of boys, a time when love and sex only existed in magical stories and movies. I thought about what Benny had said, I listened to the song again. The Teenagers, what a great word, teenager! A powerful word; our entire adolescence condensed into just three syllables. That's what songwriters are always looking for – powerful yet familiar themes – and there it was. I couldn't believe after all of our agonizing over "youth" themes, that we had overlooked such an obvious one – the teenage condition . . .

'When I arrived, I was so excited to tell Dr Luke about how I'd finally cracked the code, but he was pissed [angry]. We had spent so much time on the chorus alone that he'd banned us from spending another second on it, so I bit my tongue. We immediately began working on the verses. Katy had already mapped out some beautiful images; building forts out of tents, running away and never looking back, etc. From that we wove a beautiful story together. Finally she went in to lay down vocals, I was freaking out that I wasn't able to reveal my "Teenage Dream" version yet, and it wasn't until she had recorded the whole thing that I pulled Luke and Max aside and told them about my idea. When I sang it to them they said, "Well why didn't you say that in the first place?!" I had tried! Anyway, we re-cut the chorus and Katy was much happier with it. That was the most important thing to me. When we listened to the play back we were all so pumped that it had paid off.

I remember Max sitting back and saying, "I wish we could bottle this feeling." It was really magical.'

In truth, if ever a song title and a singer were made for each other, it was Katy and 'Teenage Dream'. She was pretty happy with the song, too. 'I wrote that song in Santa Barbara and it was a very pure moment for me, because that's where I'm from,' she told MTV News. 'And it was, like, where I started my creative juices. And also it kind of exudes this euphoric feeling because everybody remembers what their teenage dreams were – all the girls that were on your poster walls. And I want to continue to be one of those . . . teenage wet dreams. In the very beginning, I was telling the record executives, "Listen, don't tell me when it's over, don't tell me when to turn it in, don't tell me when we're out of money. I'll let you know when my gut says "Go". Because I've always followed my intuition, and that's worked for me. I'm not going to overthink that, because it's always worked for me.'

Despite the title, the song is a step forward from 'I Kissed A Girl' because it tackles the subject of adult love. Russell was the inspiration, of course, and the song is about love, commitment and giving yourself to one person. Katy herself had matured both as a person and a performer and this was now coming through in her work. 'For me it is a feeling that the title evokes,' Katy told the *Daily Record*. 'It is a song off the record and it is about someone making you feel like you are having that teenage dream about someone. Like when you are in high school and you dream about that person you want to make out

with or date. To me, this year is pretty heavy. I am going to be getting married and putting out this record, and there is so much going on that it's nice to think of those young dreams.'

On the whole, the critics loved it. 'Katy Perry aims to do for love songs in 2010 what she has already done for summer songs with "California Gurls",' said Bill Lamb on About.com. '"Teenage Dream" contains a picture perfect lyric line of the joy of falling in love. Wisely, the arrangement and vocals are understated allowing the song to work its way into the head in a fashion that is unlikely to let go soon. This is the wedding and dating song of 2010 so far.'

'Katy Perry's "Teenage Dream", the title track to her upcoming third studio album of the same name, should have her teen fans elated,' said Sara D. Anderson on AOL Radio Blog. 'Singing in falsetto, Perry innocently croons about her true love and "Valentine", who makes her feel young again, and inevitably ready to take the relationship further: "Let's go all the way tonight/No regrets, just love."'

There was a rather more scratchy review from NYmag. com. 'The title track to her new album – which, if you missed it, will feature Perry-naked-in-a-cloud-of-cotton-candy artwork – is an ode to a way-too-supporting boyfriend that, if not for a bluntly muscular chorus ('You! . . . make! . . . me!'), is nearly a ballad,' it said. 'We'd parse it for specific references to Russell Brand if we weren't aware this, like most of Perry's material, was presumably written by a coldly calculating (possibly Swedish) pop mastermind

in between dips in a Scrooge McDuck money pit. Right now, it's feeling a bit too earnest, and not nearly as catchy as the follow-up single from Perry's first album ("Hot N Cold", most definitely still a jam). That said, we are now mentally preparing ourselves for its ubiquity.'

Alyssa Rosenberg, in The Atlantic, didn't like it one tiny bit. 'I realize I'm in the midst of a bout of humorlessness here, and it's just a stupid pop song,' she wrote. 'I like me some Lady Gaga, and her lyrics aren't Shakespeare either (though the nonsense chanting in "Bad Romance" has something compelling about it). But I kind of don't care. The first part of the trope in Perry's song, the whole "OMG he sees something about me that the rest of the world is too shallow to notice!" thing is simply annoying and incoherent.'

But her view was not the prevailing one. Not only was the song an enormous success – it not only got to No 1, but made No 4 on *Rolling Stone*'s Best Singles of 2010 – it also did extremely well globally, cementing Katy as the new queen of pop. The video was much less spectacular than 'California Gurls', but equally, more appropriate to the song. Directed by Yoann Lemoine, there are various shots of Katy kneeling in the sand and looking at a man wearing Speedos, then kissing a boyfriend in a hotel pool. She is then seen in a car with her boyfriend, at a party and kissing her boyfriend underwater. Given her about-to-be-married status, this was harder than it looked.

'It is gonna be completely different from "California Gurls",' Katy said in an interview on YouTube. 'With

"Teenage Dream" you'll see a very raw, almost vulnerable [side] . . . I had to wear so many less layers of makeup. I had to make out with a boy, which was very traumatizing, I was kind of mean to him. I would be the one to call cut because I was like, "Oh I can't do this!" I feel so horrible. But I know it's a job. [Russell and I] understand what our work is.' A second video showed a montage of pictures of her, still with boyfriend – she had to suffer for her art. In the meantime, The Beelzebubs, a male a cappella group, covered the song, which was subsequently used on the television show *Glee*.

The third single from *Teenage Dream* was 'Firework', written by Katy, Mikkel S. Eriksen, Tor Erik Hermansen, Sandy Wilhelm and Ester Dean and produced by Stargate and Sandy Vee. The song was about self-empowerment and Katy said it was her favourite on the album: 'People are coming back and almost adopting it as their own anthem, and it's hard, I think, to write an anthem that's not cheesy, and I hope that this could be something in that category,' she told MTV. 'I hope this could be one of those things where it's like, Yeah, I want to put my fist up and feel proud and feel strong. But I also don't want to be cheesy, it's a fine line, and I think "Firework" . . . would be like the opus or my one song – if I had to pick a song to play – 'cause it has a great beat. But it also has a fantastic message.'

The critics, for the most part, loved it, though not everyone was complimentary. The song is 'not an actively painful listen', said Slant magazine. 'Sure, the would-be inspirational lyrics are nonsensical, and the vocal lines,

which sound like they were written for someone like Leona Lewis, are well beyond Perry's capabilities, but the chorus gains some momentum and the song would work well enough in a club setting that you could forgive its otherwise glaring weaknesses.'

Bill Lamb from About.com and Allmusic chose 'Firework' among the top tracks on the album. The song 'is a towering anthem that was aimed directly at lifting self esteem,' said Bill. 'It is a straightforward, economical self-esteem anthem. The song wastes no time in getting to the point and gives razor sharp focus to its message. As a result, it is a perfect pop record being catchy, highly melodic and designed to make every listener feel good. Effervescent pop singles rarely get better than this.'

Nick Levine of Digital Spy gave the song five out of five stars. 'It's a straight up self-empowerment anthem wrapped in a Coldplay-on-poppers club banger from the Stargate team.'

The song went to No 1 and the video was another spectacular. Directed by Dave Meyers and filmed in Budapest, there was an open casting call so fans had the chance to take part, and an astonishing 38,000 replied. The film showed fireworks shooting from Katy's chest as she sang and inspired others with low self-esteem: a shy fat girl sheds her clothes and jumps in a pool; a chemotherapy patient has the courage to show herself without hair; a young boy plays magic tricks to stop himself getting attacked by thugs; a boy stops his parents from fighting — it was all good stuff.

The final single from the album, 'E.T.', was released in February 2011 and features two verses from Kanye West. Originally meant for Three 6 Mafia, Katy heard it when Max Martin and Dr Luke played it to her, and claimed it as her own, which explains why it's so different from anything she'd done before.

'I heard it and I always knew I wanted to write this futuristic, alienistic song, and they pulled it up and I was like, "Wait, I can wrap my head around this. I know this seems like a long shot, but I think I have the perfect material to put on top of this sound."' she told MTV. 'And I did, and it really worked out perfectly. It's a whole different vibe for me. It's kind of a bit harder, it does have that urban feel underneath it. I think that's why Kanye added even another layer on top of it. And it has . . . amazing . . . sonics – I mean, there's so much to it, there's a lot in the song if you really put your headphones on and sink into the song. Even teasing people with different images from *E.T.*, people are so perplexed. They're like, "Katy Perry, you're supposed to be Betty Boop! You're supposed to be wearing pink!" It's exciting to be able to push my audience, to be like, "There's always more, I've got all of this hidden up my sleeve that I've really longed to show people."' Whatever the reviews said, her fans evidently approved as it eventually ended up at No 1.

The single got mixed reviews, while the accompanying video, directed by Floria Sigismondi, showed Katy sporting a very different look. Elaborately made up, she plays an alien visiting a broken earth in a spaceship, where she

kisses a robot, played by Shaun Ross, who then comes to life.

'Katy Perry's latest hit "E.T." – the Number One single on Billboard's Hot 100 chart this week – may be named after Steven Spielberg's adorable Eighties space alien, but its video has more to do with grim modern sci-fi,' noted Matthew Perpetua. 'In fact, the clip looks as though it could be the trailer for either a sequel to *Avatar* or a Katy Perry video game. It's a bold move away from Perry's usual silliness and sexuality, but the song itself is too – it sounds more like Evanescence's hard rock balladry than her cheerful radio hits "California Gurls" and "Teenage Dream".'

Katy said the song was about dating a foreigner (which Russell is) and the lyrics are rather different from any of her other tracks: 'You're not like the others/Futuristic lover/Different DNA.' But she wasn't just dating a foreigner: she was about to marry him, and now the time had come to tie the knot.

Wedding Belle

Given their flamboyance as a couple, there was never going to be the slightest chance that Katy and Russell would have a low-key wedding, and so it proved to be. Although they would try their utmost to keep it private, major celebrations were on the cards, and they couldn't hide everything from the world's media. In late October, Katy and Russell were snapped arriving in Jaipur, where they would get married in front of eighty-five guests in the luxury resort of Aman-i-Khás after several days of partying.

Guests included Jonathan Ross and his wife Jane Goldman, David Baddiel and David Walliams and his wife Lara. The fabled LA wedding planner Mindy Weiss, who also included Heidi Klum and Gwen Stefani among her clients, was in charge of the plans. Even the wedding invitations were out of this world: they were designed by the American street artist Shepard Fairey, who was also one of the guests. He became internationally famous after designing an iconic election poster for Barack Obama and he also designed the cover of Russell's book *My Booky Wook 2*. Katy's family was there in force, but only Russell's mother attended – his father was not invited.

Katy was a good-looking bride, and her family as a

whole looked great. A couple of months previously, Katy had used her growing wealth to treat her mother to a face-lift, and her father's reaction to it – as good-humoured and proud as it was possible to be – spoke volumes about the Hudson household. 'My daughter, little Katy Perry, bought my wife a facelift. Hallelujah! My Lord, does she look good. It's amazing what they can do. They took twenty-five years off her. I am serious – it's amazing,' he said at The Way Family Church in Temecula, California. 'I don't know how I am going to handle this. I mean, she doesn't look like her mother no more, she looks like Katy Perry's sister. It's going to be difficult because they're going to say, "Who's this old man with Katy Perry and her sister?"' The strength of the Hudsons' marriage was clear and set a great example for the younger crowd.

In the run-up to the nuptials, the couple drew up rules that had to be adhered to within their marriage, and while this was said to be Katy's idea, the ordinances affected them both. Neither was allowed to go to a nightclub with-out the other; they had to speak on the phone every day before 11p.m. Neither of them was allowed to get too drunk – given that Russell had given up drinking years earlier, this one clearly only applied to Katy – and contact with fans was only to be a photo and autograph. No kiss-ing was allowed.

Despite a huge amount of speculation about the state of their relationship, which endures to this day, both of them were certain they'd found the person they wanted to be with for the rest of their lives. 'I always knew I wanted a great

man of God, someone who was going to be an inspiration for people and also be a lovely husband and father,' Katy said in an interview with *Harper's Bazaar* before the wedding and published in December 2010 with Katy on the cover. 'We're at different places in our lives, but we can still grow together. He's thought-provoking, articulate, a real advocate. I also definitely wanted to have a laugh. I have all that in him.' She certainly seemed to appreciate his humour. Considering American and British humour is supposed to be very different, it was the cornerstone of their relationship and Katy has talked constantly about how much Russell makes her laugh.

For all the flamboyance of the ceremony, however, the wedding was to be kept a private matter – as much as possible anyway. There were to be no major magazine deals, no multi-million-pound tie-ups and no reams of coverage in the glossies. Despite their fame, the pair were, after all, just a couple in love who wanted to spend the rest of their lives together, no more, no less. Russell even said as much in *The New York Times'* Times Talks Q&A. 'We just love each other and we want to get married in front of our friends and family and keep it very normal. It ain't about selling the pictures, it ain't about doing no pre-nup, it's just a normal thing. I'm trying to preserve it, to keep it a beautiful thing. I think people get the wrong idea on how we want the wedding to play out. Love between two people is the most spectacular, yet ordinary thing in the world.'

The duo seemed uncharacteristically nervous as they arrived in Jaipur, and as they walked through the airport,

Katy attempted to cover her head with a coat – it seemed that, despite their best efforts, the strain of being under the media microscope was beginning to tell. Once in situ, however, the fun began. Russell was spotted covered in a traditional Indian henna tattoo, and he and some of the guests went to nearby Ranthambore National Park to do a safari drive. According to Indian custom, Katy was also covered with *mehndi* – henna tattoos – with the groom's initials hidden somewhere within the design, whilst sporting an Indian nose ring.

Given that she had organized the hen party, there was some surprise that Rihanna wasn't present – indeed, she had been expected to be maid of honour. It was said that recording commitments – she was working on *Loud* – had kept her away, but there was speculation from an unnamed source that she didn't think Katy was doing the right thing and so didn't want to be present to give her blessing.

'Rihanna told Katy she didn't think she should go through with it,' said the source. 'She said she couldn't be a part of Katy's wedding since she absolutely doesn't approve. Rihanna and Russell are very rarely photographed together because she doesn't think he's good enough for Katy. She just doesn't get the attraction. She was trying to go along with things even though she thinks Russell is bad news, but she reached breaking point when Katy and Russell had a fight just before the hen do. Rihanna told Katy how she felt. She's watched her get upset, she's witnessed the effects of the pair's arguments and seen Katy cancel the wedding twice.' Whether or not this is true is question-

able, though, since Katy and Russell have always given every impression of being devoted to one another.

Despite the rumours, Katy and Russell were determined to carry off the wedding in style. To begin with, there was to be a *lagna*, or engagement ceremony, followed by seven days of activities. Despite their best attempts to keep it secret, details eventually leaked out: Indian dress was the order of the day, with Katy and Russell providing saris and turbans for their guests. There were plenty of things for the couple and their guests to enjoy, including a dance tent, a hookah lounge tent and daily activities. There were dinners around the campfire and musicians, fire-eaters, snake charmers, drummers and dancers to entertain them.

Perez Hilton – who wasn't there – managed to find one guest at the wedding who was willing to talk, on condition of anonymity, and who revealed just how spectacular it had been. 'The only bummer to the wedding is that it was so hot in India and they had all the tents air conditioned, so a lot of people got sick from going in and out of the heat and cold,' he said. 'They had no band and no performer at the wedding, just a deejay. One of the cutest things is that Russell rode into the ceremony on an elephant, but there was another elephant walking beside his because apparently they're fraternal twins and can't be separated or else they'll both have panic attacks.' In total, the wedding procession was said to consist of twenty-one camels, as well as elephants, horses and traditional dancers and musicians. The only unwelcome guest at the

celebrations was a tiger that got too close to the hotel and had to be chased off by local guards.

Despite the spectacle, the couple were deeply moved, and Russell confessed afterwards that he'd nearly been in tears. He gave his new wife a ruby ring, and although Katy was wearing traditional Indian clothes in the run-up to the wedding, during the ceremony itself, she changed into a dove grey Elie Saab haute couture dress with lace sleeves.

Afterwards, the family issued a short and dignified statement: 'The very private and spiritual ceremony, attended by the couple's closest family and friends, was performed by a Christian minister and longtime friend of the Hudson family. The backdrop was the inspirational and majestic countryside of northern India.'

As the celebrations began to wind down, Rihanna gave an interview in which she point-blank denied boycotting the wedding. Equally, however, she was less than forthcoming in her endorsement of Russell as groom. 'He was interviewing me on TV,' she told the *Daily Star*. 'I was ill and it was the worst interview I'd ever done. I was throwing up in a bucket and nothing was funny to me. I thought it was the most stupid fucking interview I ever did in my life. Why am I talking to this idiot? He made me want to throw up again.

'It was a stupid interview. [But] we did another interview and I realized he was funny. I was probably a complete bitch, but only months afterwards did I get it [the relationship between Katy and Russell]. He's crazy but it took a while for the penny to drop that they were perfect for each other.'

After the wedding the couple jetted off on honeymoon, taking a helicopter out to the airport and then chartering a flight to the Maldives, where they stayed at the Soneva Fushi resort. There were reports that Katy had imposed a month-long sex ban before the wedding, so they could enjoy the honeymoon even more, and that Katy was bitten by a spider on the honeymoon and given medication that ruled out sex. The story was never clarified and it's difficult to know how it got out in the first place, but it's probably safe to assume that all those people who had forecast the wedding would never happen were simply looking for some gossip to suggest there was trouble in paradise, when in fact the married couple were perfectly happy.

Now that they were married, there was intense speculation about when they would start a family. It was plainly on the cards at some stage, but when? Both had exceedingly busy careers, and Katy was about to start touring again, but the two of them made no secret about what they wanted in the long term. In an interview given just before the wedding, Katy spoke about the couple's desire to have children. 'When we start, Russell won't want to stop,' she said. 'He will actually make a very good dad. He really loves kids. I am just concerned about how many he will try and make me have. It wouldn't shock me if he tried to go into double figures. His dream is to have eleven boys and name them after the West Ham team.' Perhaps not just yet, though.

Fittingly, given the circumstances of their courtship, Katy and Russell's first public appearance as man and wife

came at the MTV Europe Music Awards in Madrid in November 2010. Katy looked stunning in a Jeremy Scott 'Admit One' red sequinned minidress teamed with blue Sergio Rossi platforms, and both looked besottedly happy as they sported matching gold wedding rings. Katy performed that night and was nominated for five awards; in the event she took home only one – Best Video for 'California Gurls' – but two things were clear: the couple were clearly utterly happy in their married life and it was business as usual, with both of them getting on with their respective careers.

Russell gave his first interview since the wedding to *Loose Women*, and he took the opportunity to emphasize that underneath it all they were just like everyone else. 'It was just normal. It's like a normal wedding,' he protested. 'Everyone gets all worked up about showbiz and celebrity, but other than the bit where you're on the telly or you're singing a song, it's normal. It's just a normal marriage.'

And did he give Katy a tiger as a gift, as some people had alleged? 'I'm a vegetarian. You don't give people tigers; it's stupid, it's dangerous and the tigers don't like it,' he replied.

And so the merry-go-round began again. Katy appeared on the catwalk of a Victoria's Secret fashion show, while Russell thoroughly enjoyed portraying himself as the put-upon husband. 'We're getting ready to go somewhere and she went, "You're wearing that shirt, are you?" I wasn't allowed to wear it.' It was an act he went on to repeat many

times, delighting in making the point that it was Katy who wore the trousers. Inevitably, people took this at face value and speculated that the marriage was in trouble, but nothing of the sort was the case. Katy played up to it too, however, claiming that she kept a naughty and nice chart for Russell pinned to the fridge door. 'He gets gold stars when he behaves to earn him treats,' she said.

Katy, meanwhile, continued her promotional work for 'Firework', although when she performed it at the BBC Radio 1 Teen Awards in London, she broke down in the middle of it, overcome by emotion. 'I meet a lot of people every day from all different backgrounds all around the world but I've never met people who touched me in this way,' she told the *Daily Star* afterwards. 'I have a tendency to get sidetracked by trends, by the words, by commercials or what people think I should be, and swept away with everything. But I feel like it's days like this that help me get back to the person I should be. It's good to feel like I'm not doing anything in vain and that people listen to me. Teenagers often feel awkward or like they don't have a voice. When I was a teenager I didn't live in the moment – I just looked past it. I often still feel like a teenager sometimes so I can identify with them. These kids have a voice to speak and be a role model to other kids, that's why the Teen Awards are so important. As a young adult who still feels like a teenager, I am inspired by them. I was emotional before I sang "Firework". I got chills and butterflies – it's a huge adrenaline rush. All the hairs stick up on my body and sometimes I don't even have to sing

because the crowds sing it louder. I still feel nervous performing to crowds. It's not that I don't feel ready but I worry that they'll rush the stage as they're all screaming my name or I feel like a wanna yack!'

There was no let up in either of their schedules, however. Katy and Russell were pictured at the premiere of Russell's latest film, *The Tempest*, in LA, and with them on the red carpet was Helen Mirren, who was also Russell's co-star in the remake of *Arthur*. Russell sparked pregnancy rumours by touching Katy's stomach, but in truth the pair simply couldn't keep their hands off one another.

In a television interview with Ellen DeGeneres, Katy revealed that yes, she was thinking of changing her name to Russell's. She then provoked the audience into raptures when Ellen told her that Helen Mirren had a crush on Russell. 'She needs to step off my man,' said Katy, looking pretty sanguine and assured. 'Actually, I kind of don't mind that someone else takes part of the responsibility because it's a lot of work . . . There's never a dull moment.' Katy also revealed the real secret behind their relationship: 'We're just really good friends. We have three cats and we just like being at home with our cats and having fun.' The wild Russell of old had evidently grown up. While Katy wasn't exactly putting herself forward as a wild child – staying at home and taking her husband's name were, after all, pretty traditional things to do – it showed how Katy's background was coming to the fore: she was still the nice girl she'd always been.

A couple of days later, Google published its Zeitgeist

list of the most Googled people in the world and Katy was on it. Russell was also getting his fair share of accolades: the US edition of *Cosmopolitan* voted him the year's sexiest bad boy, adding that he was the 'Fun, Fearless Male of the Year'.

In private, Katy was now calling herself Katy Brand. And when she gave an interview to *Grazia* magazine, she hinted at a very spicy love life. 'I have secrets and magic tricks, of course [in the bedroom],' she said. 'I can't share them because then you'd all know. But let's just say I'm not shy. And I never wear sweats. Ever. I make sure we have time [for each other]. We're both busy but this is a huge part of my life. I call the shots on my schedule. I put in breaks. There are weekends for Russ and weekends for me and my friends. Neither of us ever wants to lose ourself or the other in fame. Every day he amazes me. He makes me laugh like no one else. We are each other's perfect match.'

There was just a moment of frostiness when Russell posted a rather unflattering picture of his new missus on Twitter. Katy was used to everyone thinking of her as extremely glamorous, but this picture seemed to have been taken immediately after she'd woken up, and she had no make-up on, lifeless hair and a rather gloomy expression. The shot wasn't up there for long, though: it disappeared after only a couple of hours. For once, Russell's sense of humour seemed to have gone too far.

That was perhaps the catalyst for new claims that the marriage was in trouble at the beginning of the year,

when stories emerged that they were seeking marriage guidance – claims that were totally and emphatically denied. In truth, the couple were on a roll, happily married and with everything to live for. The really big news in Katy's life was that she was about to start a new tour . . .

California Dreams

Katy and Russell were settling down in two places: their main home, an estate near LA's Griffith Park, complete with a three-car garage which Katy painted pink and turned into a closet; and a smaller apartment in New York. However, there was work to be done. Katy might have taken Russell's name and been getting ready to have his babies, but she also had an album to promote and a career to sustain, and now it was time for her second major tour. The California Dreams tour was due to kick off in February 2011 and would continue until November 2011, taking in Europe, Australasia, Asia and the Americas.

'I hope that it's going to engage all of your senses: sight, sound, smell, taste, touch,' she said during the VMAs. Previously she had explained, 'I guess I'm looking forward to making music videos on this new album . . . and I'm really excited about incorporating the look and the idea of some of the songs on tour and making a massive production of it. I'm gonna want a lot of visuals. I want it to be ten times better than when I was on tour last.'

It was a sign of how far Katy had come that she could call on the very best acts to support her, too. It would be 'super girl power', said Katy as she announced a decidedly international female line-up to open for her: the Swedish

singer-songwriter Robyn, the French band Yelle, the Welsh singer-songwriter Marina & the Diamonds, the New Zealand singer-songwriter Zowie and the American singer-songwriter Janelle Monáe.

The only fly in the ointment was a spat with Calvin Harris, which seemed to have been brewing for some time. Calvin had originally been mentioned in connection with Katy's album *Teenage Dreams*, but in the event did not participate. He was then named as part of the tour's line-up in the UK and Ireland, but dropped out. Katy was not pleased.

The state of play between the two was revealed via an exchange on Twitter when Katy tweeted, 'FYI ALL UK & IRELAND RELATED SHOWS @CalvinHarris will NOT be joining in on the fun and has CANCELLED last minute.'

Calvin responded, 'Sorry to all who wanted to see me with Katy – her team suddenly moved the goalposts, and I was to appear on stage with no production. It would have looked s**t, sounded s**t – trust me you would have been more disappointed SEEING the show than u are with me cancelling. That's the honest truth. Her show is AWESOME, you'll all have an amazing time without me. (especially w/o me DJing on a cardboard box in front of a pink curtain).'

Katy did not take this lying down: '. . . funny the goal post seems to be perfectly fine for New Young Pony Club, Yelle, Robyn, Marina & the Diamonds to name a few. Or

how bout Janelle Monae and her 16 piece band . . . etc . . . it's fine, I'm used to you cancelling on me, it's become ur staple!'

Calvin tried to build bridges: 'I am really sorry @katy-perry I'm just upset because I really wanted to play but ur team made it impossible. We tried really hard to sort it out, but playing side of stage for 30 mins, it seemed pointless me even being there. Didn't intend to cause offence or upset anybody.'

In the event, the DJ Skeet Skeet took his place.

Calvin wasn't the only one to be cancelling appearances, though – Russell did the same when he pulled out of receiving an award for outstanding contribution to comedy at the British Comedy Awards, choosing to accept the accolade via a video link instead. It was explained that he was attending to a sick friend in New York, but the organizers were disappointed: not only was Jonathan Ross hosting the event (anything that brought Russell and Jonathan together still made the news) but if Russell had been there, Katy might have come, too. Her slightly reckless boast a year earlier that the two of them were becoming the new Brangelina was beginning to look as if it might be true. The couple attracted massive interest wherever they went, and Katy had become a huge star in her own right, so much so that her schedule was even more booked up than ever. As she continued to release tour dates, Katy revealed that things had become so hectic she and Russell were having to plan dates to be together up to eight months in

advance! In total, the tour was going to include ninety-five dates, with marriage breaks, as it were, being factored in along the way.

Given the lengthy times they spent apart, it's no surprise that there was continued speculation about the state of their marriage, which in reality continued to go from strength to strength. Matters weren't helped when Russell gave an interview to Piers Morgan and mused on his new married life: 'It's difficult to get used to one person, and being in the same house with them every day,' he said, not that they spent that much time in the same house. 'If she leaves stuff lying around, I have to deal with it, and if I leave stuff on the floor I have to pick it up. That confuses me. And she takes ages to get ready. It's unbelievable, I had no idea what went on, I was never normally around for that bit. I see her a lot, that's what marriage is, like it or lump it, she is always around.'

As for monogamy, Russell said, 'Like with everything, drugs, alcohol, I take it one step at a time. Of course marriage is for life, and that's what I wanted. I used to have sex twenty times a week, but now? I'm a bloody good gardener . . .!'

Russell's comments were leapt on as proof that all was not well, but Russell was just doing what he'd always done – making comedy out of his life – and what he'd actually said was that he wanted to be with Katy for ever. Despite this, there was still a small coterie of mostly young, male admirers who just couldn't bear to admit that Russell

was a tamed man. It was increasingly apparent why it suited Russell to live in the States: not only was his career based there, in America he was able to develop a new life without being constantly reminded of the one he'd left behind.

Even when they were together, both Katy and Russell worked incredibly hard. Katy was in training for her tour: 'I'm on a meal plan, which absolutely sucks,' she told the *Daily Star*. 'I'll work out, go to a vocal lesson, run through the entire set at rehearsals, go to dance rehearsal until 10pm, then sort through emails. I feel like I'm training for the Olympics.'

In February, fed up with the constant rumours about their marriage, Katy used an appearance at the Grammys to feature shots of the couple's Indian wedding: while she was lowered onto the stage on a giant swing, a video of the wedding played in the background. Katy also wore three Armani outfits for the show, each one more glamorous than the last, and made her entrance wearing giant feathered wings. She had competition on the night, however, from Rihanna, who was a knockout in a semi-sheer Jean Paul Gaultier creation, Jennifer Lopez in a Pucci minidress and Lady Gaga freshly hatched from a Hussein Chalayan egg.

That Katy was serious about seeing as much of Russell as she possibly could was evident in March when she crossed the Atlantic twice in twenty-four hours. Straight after a concert in Vienna, she caught a flight to LA, where she was briefly reunited with Russell before singing with

the group PS22 for Oprah Winfrey's post-Oscars party. She and Russell appeared blissfully happy to be together again and Katy looked remarkably fresh-faced, despite her gruelling schedule. The audience screamed with delight as she appeared on stage in a metallic gold dress, surrounded by the children in the choir: 'Did you see my missus on *Oprah*?' Russell tweeted afterwards. 'With that PS22 kids choir! So cute! So sexy! (Kids cute, missus sexy – if that needs clarifying).' And with that Katy stepped straight back onto a plane and returned to Europe to continue her tour.

Meanwhile Russell cheerfully continued to play the hen-pecked husband: 'I'm a butler. My life used to be about chaos, glass, blood, madness, but now it's, "Go and get that fridge." That's after five months. How am I going to be a decade down the road? I'll be like a servant man, polishing windows and gardening.'

Katy's star continued to shine, and on the whole her tour generated positive reviews: 'What ensues is the visual embodiment of a sugar rush, punctuated by endless saucy "ooh!" moments,' wrote Caroline Sullivan in the *Guardian*. 'A dancer dressed as a Pierrot peeks under her skirt during "Ur So Gay" – whose title is sung by the audience with discomfiting glee – she exhorts boys to throw their shirts on stage on a reconfigured, jazzy version of "I Kissed A Girl" and she even plays, oo-er, a rhinestone-encrusted flute on a cover of Jay-Z's "Big Pimpin".

'Silly as hell? Yes – but also very funny. Most of it probably goes over the crowd's heads, though. Nor are they old

enough to suspect that the lavish, Day-Glo production is probably partially influenced by the more psychedelic aspects of *The Wizard of Oz* and *Alice in Wonderland*, with Perry as the questing heroine. Did Perry's reformed-hedonist husband, Russell Brand, have a hand in that side of things? If not, he's certainly responsible for her occasional lame attempts at an English accent.'

The *NME* also highlighted the OTT element to Katy's show. 'Pretty soon after she explodes onstage in a cornea-cauterising multi-coloured starburst of sound, light and (yes) piped-in candyfloss smell, you start to get the feeling Katy Perry is treating you like a child,' wrote Emily Mackay. 'Sure, the dizzyingly brilliant title track of her second album *Teenage Dream*, tossed casually in as the opener, might be full of mature, measured adult yearning in the verses, gleefully cast aside for a gutsy rush of eternal youth in the chorus, but it's delivered from a stage that's as plastic-moulded as a Malibu Stacy Hammersmith Apollo toyset. The sugar-coated spiral staircases and cupcake podiums will over the course of the next hour or so bear a tumbling kaleidoscope of skits, graphics, dancers, mimes, swings, glitter, glitter, glitter and every candy-coated distraction Perry can employ to ensure that by the end of the night she will own your eyes like the Fourth of July.' She did, however, go on to praise Katy's voice and songs. This is what Katy does best: lay on a visual extravaganza, utilizing the themes of being a teenager. What's more, the audiences loved it and told her so.

Russell continued his Greek chorus in the background:

'I've really changed,' he lamented. 'I've given up loads of things that I was really good at. I used to Google myself all the time but I don't even do that any more and that was my favourite hobby. Katy's only gone and copied me. I'm eight months Google-free, and she's four months Google-free.' Another addiction gone.

There was, however, a frisson of concern from other quarters. Katy's mother, Mary, was said to be considering writing about her famous daughter, and put together a few thoughts that were leaked on the internet. It emerged that she wasn't quite as sanguine about her daughter as she sometimes appeared. 'Katy stepped out from behind the changing room doors in a tiny, risqué costume,' she recalled of one particular performance. 'No mother wants to see the tops of her daughter's boobs. My first instinct was to order her back behind those doors and demand she put something else on. However, I had no problem letting my eyebrows say what I wouldn't allow my mouth to utter.'

However, Mary still hoped Katy was destined to be a worship leader – a Kathryn Kuhlman type of healer: Kathryn was a Baptist faith healer before her death. 'I recognized the psalmist gift in her performance,' Mary continued. 'Yet she sang out, "I kissed a girl, and I liked it," while thousands joined her. One part of my heart soared – the other part broke for the thousands of hungry souls being fed something that didn't nourish their spirits but fed their flesh.'

She went on to muse, 'Oh dear God, how can I save her

from all this? The money, the fame, the network, the people surrounding her – how can I compete with all this?'

Katy's parents were clearly concerned, but paradoxically Katy seemed to be in safe hands with Russell. More besotted with his wife than ever, Russell might not have stopped his public musings on how much his life had changed, but he was clearly devoted to Katy, and very protective. Whilst Katy had always been anti-drugs, thanks to Russell she didn't spend a great deal of time drinking alcohol either, so at least some of the temptations that blight so many promising careers didn't look like they would put her in harm's way.

Given her chosen profession, Katy's parents couldn't have given her a better start in life. As well as courage, confidence and a sense of self-worth, they gave her love and security, and while they were concerned about some aspects of her music career, they have always stood by and supported her. They also get on well with Russell and understand, where so many have failed to, that his past life is just that – in the past.

Katy has scaled heights that would have seemed unimaginable just a short time ago. Not only does she have a successful singing career, she has become a style icon, a frequent cover girl on the glossiest of magazines, and is sought after by designers wanting her to wear their clothes. She sells records in their hundreds of thousands, can sell out an auditorium, has boys fancying her and girls wanting to emulate her. It's quite an act to pull off.

What's more, her career looks set to continue to soar.

Katy's put hard work into it, dedication and talent, and her husband is so devoted that he told Piers Morgan that making movies with Tom Cruise would come second to being married to Katy. The two of them have the world at their feet, and the only way is up.